IN-CLASS FLIP

A Student-Centered Approach to Differentiated Learning

Martha A. Ramírez and Carolina R. Buitrago

International Society for Technology in Education

PORTLAND, OREGON • ARLINGTON, VIRGINIA

In-Class Flip
A Student-Centered Approach to Differentiated Learning

Martha A. Ramírez and Carolina R. Buitrago

Director of Books and Journals: *Colin Murcray*
Acquisitions Editor: *Valerie Witte*
Editor: *Emily Reed*
Copy Editor: *Courtney Burkholder*
Proofreader: *Lisa Hein*
Indexer: *Wendy Allex*
Book Design and Production: *Jeff Puda*
Figure design and interior artwork: *David Beltrán*
Cover Design: *Christina DeYoung*

Library of Congress Cataloging-in-Publication Data

Names: Ramirez, Martha, author. | Rodriguez Buitrago, Carolina, author.
Title: In-class flip : a student-centered approach to differentiated
  learning / Martha Ramirez and Carolina Rodriguez Buitrago.
Description: First edition. | Portland, Oregon : International Society for
  Technology in Education, 2022. | Includes bibliographical references and
  index.
Identifiers: LCCN 2022008704 | ISBN 9781564849588 (paperback) | ISBN
  9781564849595 (epub) | ISBN 9781564849601 (pdf)
Subjects: LCSH: Flipped classrooms. | Individualized instruction. |
  Student-centered learning.
Classification: LCC LB1029.F55 R36 2022 | DDC 371.39/4—dc23/eng/20220419
LC record available at https://lccn.loc.gov/2022008704

First Edition
ISBN: 978-1-56484-958-8
Ebook version available

Printed in the United States of America
ISTE® is a registered trademark of the International Society for Technology in Education.

About ISTE

The International Society for Technology in Education (ISTE) is home to a passionate community of global educators who believe in the power of technology to transform teaching and learning, accelerate innovation, and solve tough problems in education.

ISTE inspires the creation of solutions and connections that improve opportunities for all learners by delivering: practical guidance, evidence-based professional learning, virtual networks, thought-provoking events, and the ISTE Standards. ISTE is also the leading publisher of books focused on technology in education. For more information or to become an ISTE member, visit iste.org. Subscribe to ISTE's YouTube channel and connect with ISTE on Twitter, Facebook, and LinkedIn.

Related ISTE Titles

To see all books available from ISTE, please visit iste.org/books.

About the Authors

Martha Ramírez (@martharamirezco) is a teacher educator, English professor and academic consultant in Bogotá, Colombia. She has a bachelor's degree in foreign languages from Universidad Pedagogica Nacional and a master's degree in education from the Universidad de Los Andes. She is a master teacher of Flipped Learning Global Initiative (FLGI), one of the experts in both the Flipped Learning Level II course and the FLGI differentiation certification course. She served as a volunteer coordinator of Electronic Village Online (EVO; TESOL initiative) for four years and has been a virtual moderator of the Flipped Learning EVO session since 2016. Martha has participated in several flipped learning national and international projects, including Universidad de Los Andes, Universidad Externado, Pontificia Universidad Católica de Ecuador, and University of Oregon. Currently, Martha is part of Bilingualism and Multilingualism research group of Universidad de los Andes, doing research in Growth Mentality where she applies flipped learning as part of her research projects.

Carolina R. Buitrago (@crbuitrago) has been an EFL teacher for over 20 years. She currently works as a full-time professor and researcher at Institución Universitaria Colombo Americana–UNICA. Carolina is a master teacher for Flipped Learning Global Initiative and was mentioned as one of the FLGI 50 (the top 50 Flipped Learning leaders in higher education worldwide) in 2018. Carolina is also one of the 49 international delegates that participated in the revision and evaluation of the Global Standards for Flipped Learning. Carolina co-led the project: "Flipping English learning, improving our 21st Century Colombian learners' outcomes through technology and autonomy," which won the BETT Education and Technology in Higher Education Award at the BETT LATAM Leadership Summit 2015. She is a master teacher of FLGI, one of the experts in both the Flipped Learning Level II course and the FLGI lesson planning certification course. She served as a volunteer coordinator of EVO for three years and was a virtual moderator of the Flipped Learning EVO session between 2015 and 2020. Carolina led the team in charge of planning and delivering FlipTech Latam 2019. She has been a member of the board of the Flipped Learning Network since 2021.

Acknowledgments

Writing this book has been like a road trip! It has been so much fun, with its unexpected turns, smooth, fast roads, and bumpy detours. We have learned more in this process than we could ever share in the contents within. We would like to start by thanking Jon Bergmann—flipped learning pioneer and author—for finding the value in our work and inviting us to share it with the world. A huge thanks to Jeannette Smith for her knowledge and incredible contributions to the editing of this book. A special thanks to all of the incredible educators who shared their voices and contributed to our own understanding of how the in-class flip can be applied in different contexts around the world: Dr. Gwo-Jen Hwang, Heath Chittenden, Kate Baker, Alexa Finck, Paola Cardona, Jeff Magoto, Randy Brown, Katie Lanier, Antonio BernabéuPellús, Steve Griffiths, Cara Johnson Allen, Rebeka Cerqua, Kyle Niemis, Jake Habegger, Jeremy Cumming, Susan White, and Daniel Lumsden.

Many thanks to our flipped learning tribe for your unconditional support, opinions, and constant feedback; to our colleagues and friends Juliana Diaz and Diana Salazar for brainstorming ideas with us when inspiration came up short; and to Camila Velasco for giving us the final push we needed to make this book a reality. Her dedication, organization, and hard work helped us move the needle towards completion.

Thanks to David Beltrán, our graphic designer, for reading our minds and illustrating our work beautifully; to Maria Ramírez and Ricardo Ramírez for their inspiration and motivational words at just the right moment; and to Carlo Granados and Robyn Brinks-Lockwood, early readers of the document—your feedback was very valuable. Thank you to all of the people who knowingly or unknowingly inspired us to move forward. And thanks to you, reader, for believing in our message and for buying our book. We hope you enjoy it.

Dedication

To David, whose unconditional love and support is embedded in so much of the work put into this book. To my grandpa, Hugo, whom I wish was here to see my first published book. —**Martha**

For Iván, Luciana, and Jacobo: the engines of my life and the support I need to be me. Thanks for teaching me about myself and empowering me to put my voice out there in the world. And for my grandma, Argelia Sabogal: thanks for teaching me to reach for the stars. —**Carolina**

Contents

Foreword

IN A RECENT CONVERSATION WITH A PUBLISHER IN THE MIDDLE EAST,
he shared that he has seen a huge increase in the conversation about flipped learning.
He surmised that the COVID-19 pandemic forced educators to evaluate how and what
they are teaching. Further, he said that few teachers in his region wanted to return to
the same old way of teaching that they did before the pandemic.

I too have seen a growing interest in flipped learning as a result of the pandemic. There
has been a resurgence of interest in flipped learning globally. Though flipped learning
solved many of the problems when schools went remote, the pandemic also revealed
to us many of the systemic problems in our educational system. It is as if the pandemic
amplified what was broken and showed us that we need a better way to teach. Many
teachers had the realization that once they returned to a more "normal" school, things
would have to be different. One group of teachers who were best prepared to move to
remote and online learning were those who had implemented flipped learning into
their classes. One teacher on Twitter summed it up when he said something like, The
Pandemic: What every #FlippedLearning teacher has been preparing for, for the last
ten years.

Two of those teachers who have been preparing are Martha Ramírez and Carolina R.
Buitrago, the authors of this book. I first encountered them on Twitter around 2016.
Martha had published an article about the in-class flip, and I remember scouring it
and referencing her material in all my presentations. I recognized their unique twist
on flipped learning as a solution for many teachers, those with access issues, students
who struggle with the content, schools where homework is not an option, and complex topics that needed special attention.

I reached out to Martha and we connected. She then quickly introduced me to the
other half of her cohort, Carolina. Since that time the three of us have collaborated
on a variety of projects. They have been my go-to experts for everything related to the
in-class flip. In fact, we debated about what to call what they are doing. I did a number
of Zoom interviews with them and used their work to help other teachers across the
globe to hear about how they can use flipped learning to change the way they teach.

I was the invited keynote speaker at a conference in Colombia that Martha was also
a part of, with a workshop right after. I quickly realized that Martha was the real star

so I stepped back and let her do her thing. The teachers in the workshop were mesmerized by her intensely practical approach to teaching and learning, and I know they learned a whole lot more from her than they did from me. She understood the context of Colombian education and she understood their struggles. As you read this book you will discover what I have found in working with Martha and Carolina—they get your struggles and know how to help you with some of the biggest challenges in your classes, namely differentiation. We all struggle with students of different abilities and backgrounds. Martha and Carolina not only understand this, they also know how to help you solve this problem.

Though I had spoken about the in-class flip many times, I hadn't used it myself until just recently. Now that I am back in the classroom, I have found that I must add elements of the in-class flip into my flipped mastery classes. The elements that I gleaned from this book and Martha and Carolina's work making me a better teacher.

The in-class flip and many other elements are spelled out in super-practical terms in this book. This book isn't just a good read, it's a guide on how you can transform your class and do real, extreme differentiation. If you are looking for a book where you can use what you learn right after you read a section, then this is the book for you! It is heavy on application and yet still makes a compelling case for why you should consider this amazing approach. Their passion for teaching and learning jumps off of the pages. You are in for quite a ride.

—**JON BERGMANN,** Teacher, flipped learning pioneer, and author of several books, including the best-selling *Flip Your Classroom*

Our Path to Discovering the In-Class Flip Model

AFTER TEACHING FOR MORE THAN FIFTEEN YEARS and understanding the importance of continued growth in our teaching practice, we stumbled upon the concept of the in-class flip via the internet. We had both been looking for ways to innovate and improve our teaching . . . and there it was! A new pedagogical model, the in-class flip, explained in a YouTube video.

Martha was the head of a languages department at a bilingual school at the time. I was teaching at a master's program online. We both remember well the moment we encountered the concept of the in-class flip. I was holding my newborn baby while browsing on my smartphone; Martha was connected to an online flipped learning session (where I was a moderator). One of my co-moderators, Kevin Coleman, shared the link to Jennifer Gonzalez's Edutopia blog post titled "Modifying the Flipped Classroom, the 'In-Class' Version". That post introduced us to this alternate way of flipping the classroom.

How Twitter Changed Our Lives

We are both strong believers in the importance of sharing and collaborating with fellow educators. It's a way to encounter different perspectives on how to improve teaching practices. So we both opened Twitter accounts and started microblogging. Microblogging became a way to reflect on and share our personal teaching experiences—our successes, failures, and reflections—with an online community of teachers committed to constructing better ways of teaching. Twitter gave us a voice and a gateway to finding a "tribe" of educators who understand and support our educational perspectives. We started tweeting like crazy, sharing posts, videos, pictures of our classrooms, and teaching ideas based on flipped learning. Little did we know, one of those tweets appeared in Jon Bergmann's feed. We had previously discussed the idea of writing a book; Twitter became the gateway for this project to become a reality.

What Will This Book Do for You?

We hope this book will inspire you to explore new ideas and strategies, and to use the tools we suggest to plan and teach via your own in-class flips. As in-class flip enthusiasts, we have tested a multitude of possible scenarios, and we haven't always been successful.

To help you avoid repeating our mistakes, in this book we've created a list of lessons:

- We provide a definition for the in-class flip.

- We identify configurations for doing station work.

- We share different types of stations, and alternatives for those who don't want to use stations in class.

- We give tips for lesson planning.

We have no doubt that you and your students will experience many benefits from the information we provide. In advancing flipped learning, we will share what educators are doing in other countries. We will demonstrate that flipped learning is not static and explore how it is evolving thanks to research, classroom innovation, and technology. With this book, we want to contribute to classroom innovation and research in the flipped learning field as our work has inspired teachers in Colombia to carry out formal research on the in-class flip strategy.

We hope this book transforms your teaching as much as the in-class flip has changed ours. After reading this book, we don't believe your classrooms will be the same. You will discover your own potential and that of your students. We invite you to take flipped learning to a whole new level.

How to Get the Most out of This Book

This book was written by two passionate teachers who want to work with educators who are struggling to plan active, student-centered lessons, and who want to create a positive change in their classrooms. The book is separated into twelve chapters and an appendix to give you an overall view of the in-class flip and how we apply this method of teaching.

Here is what you will find in each chapter:

- Chapter 1 defines the in-class flip along with an analysis of flipped learning, in-class flipping, and blended learning.

- Chapter 2 presents twenty reasons why you should try out the in-class flip. If you are not convinced the in-class flip is for you, then this chapter will help you take the plunge.

- Chapter 3 analyzes in-situ (non-station) work. We've discovered that with certain instructional structures, we can create in-class flip experiences without using stations.

- Chapter 4 shows the station configurations and examples to use when you incorporate the in-class flip.

- Chapter 5 walks you through the "how." We show you the different types of stations we have developed and what you will need to prepare your classroom.

- Chapter 6 looks at the in-class flip as a powerful way to differentiate instruction. We share our own practical ways to do so as well as teacher cases for you to consider. Who knows? You may find the right approach to address your own differentiated learning situation.

- Chapter 7 examines planning for an in-class flip in detail. We share our experiences and different techniques for designing our own in-class flips. We even share our own notes, sketches, and formats to help you begin! If you are task-oriented, you will appreciate the checklist included in this chapter, so you don't miss any details while planning your lessons.

- Chapter 8 explores planning content for an in-class flip.

- Chapter 9 offers you our ten tips to get started. These are the main ideas we wished we had known when we embarked on this adventure.

- Chapter 10 provides a brief but juicy look into how we assess in our in-class flip implementations.

- Chapter 11 discusses how to overcome the most common problems with the in-class flip. It also addresses practical ways to clear these hurdles.

- Chapter 12 presents our favorite technologies for creating and delivering in-class flip materials.

- Chapter 13 provides ways for you to take your flipped and in-class flipped environments up a notch by rewiring your teaching approach. We demonstrate how you can use different approaches (content- and language--integrated learning, project-based learning, mastery learning, gamification, and online learning) with your in-class flip.

- The book's appendix offers a "grab and go" menu. If you want to find a more detailed summary of each chapter and quick reference for specific topics, this is the place to go.

Throughout the book, we've added some valuable stories from in-class flippers around the world. Many teachers have shared their expertise in their unique in-class flip approaches. We distributed an online feedback survey and received teacher responses from New Zealand, Australia, the United States, Taiwan, Canada, and, of course, Colombia.

What makes this book exceptional is that the wisdom and experience of fellow educators around the world corroborate our own experiences with the in-class flip. So we invite you to pay close attention to the stories in the Teaching Spotlight sections of this book. Their voices have also been featured in the In-class Flip around the World sections.

We have also added some Reflective Pauses so you can think and reflect on the issues discussed in the book and personalize its contents. We have included some QR codes that lead you to many resources, either our own, or those of our contributors. We encourage you to check them out.

You may read the book from cover to cover, or just dig into the chapters you are more drawn to. Use the appendix and index to find specific topics or answers to your questions. We also invite you to follow us on Twitter if you don't already, and to share your feedback on the book and how it has informed your practice. We hope you enjoy reading our book as much as we enjoyed writing it!

Martha (@martharamirezco)
Carolina (@crbuitrago)

CHAPTER 1

Rewiring Our Flipped Classrooms through the In-Class Flip

This chapter addresses several ISTE Standards:

2.1 Learner

Educators continually improve their practice by learning from and with others and exploring proven and promising practices that leverage technology to improve student learning. Educators:

a. Set professional learning goals to explore and apply pedagogical approaches made possible by technology and reflect on their effectiveness.

2.5 Designer

Educators design authentic, learner-driven activities and environments that recognize and accommodate learner variability. Educators:

b. Design authentic learning activities that align with content area standards and use digital tools and resources to maximize active, deep learning.

2.6 Facilitator

Educators facilitate learning with technology to support student achievement of the ISTE Standards for Students. Educators:

a. *Foster a culture where students take ownership of their learning goals and outcomes in both independent and group settings.*

b. *Manage the use of technology and student learning strategies in digital platforms, virtual environments, hands-on makerspaces or in the field.*

d. *Model and nurture creativity and creative expression to communicate ideas, knowledge or connections.*

OLGA IS A PUBLIC-SCHOOL TEACHER IN COLOMBIA. She has forty-five students in her eighth-grade EFL writing class. She has tried to flip her class, but without success. Approximately thirty percent of her students never watch the videos, and twenty percent of them must work in the afternoon with their parents, as extra labor. So, they don't have the time or support to do homework. Adding to that, one of Olga's students is deaf, and Olga hasn't had any formal training on how to deal with his disability. Olga provides direct instruction in class, but she feels she's only reaching about forty percent of her students due to many poor results in writing assessments.

Jose is a struggling student in a middle-school class in New Mexico. He doesn't have easy access to the internet, and his science teacher just started flipping his class. So now Jose struggles even more since he has to go to internet cafes or his friends' homes to watch the videos for class. When he can finally access the videos, he takes notes by stopping the videos and copying every word that comes out of the teacher's mouth. Jose is ready to throw in the towel and tell his dad he wants to change schools.

Yu-Hung is a math teacher in a private high school in China, with twenty-six students in his classroom. His is an international school, with students from diverse cultural and ethnic backgrounds. Registrations are open all year long. Students come from different parts of the world with varied educational settings. While most students do take the required English courses, Yu-Hung also has to manage students' difficulties adapting to Chinese culture, language barriers, and subject matter limitations—all in the same setting.

Olga, Jose, and Yu-Hung are among the classroom teachers and students all over the world who experience many difficulties every day. Teaching and learning are messy. They involve a set of variables that make the experience challenging and thorny. However, engaging your curiosity and changing your mindset can lead to high levels of student engagement and deeper learning. Keep reading to see how we changed our mindset and went beyond the flipped classroom for our students' benefit. Our ideas may help Olga, Jose, and Yu-Hung—why not you, too?

How the In-Class Flip Came into the Picture

As we describe in the introduction, we came across a video (first aired in 2014) by Jennifer Gonzalez, who explained that an in-class flip was an alternative flipped learning approach. Students could access the flipped content at a station setting within the classroom walls. We found great relevance in this innovation, so we started exploring further. We searched for what other educators were saying about the in-class flip method and found the following information:

- Jon Bergmann and Aaron Sams (2015) called it the "in-flip." They shared positive teacher experiences in their book *Flipped Learning for Elementary Instruction*.

- In her blog, Catlin Tucker (2016) said that the in-class flip contained "the benefits of the flipped classroom [embedded] into the station rotation model." She has been recognized for her work with blended learning.

- Mark Barnes and Jennifer Gonzalez (2015) asserted that the in-class flip was a new way to flip when the homework flip was falling apart.

We realized that the in-class flip had become a valid strategy for teachers who couldn't flip their content outside of class for a variety of reasons. It became part of our teaching practice.

I (Martha) had been flipping my classes for a couple of years and was finding it hard to flip my lessons with my literature class due to a strict school homework policy that restricted the amount of time students could devote to homework every day. So when this new option appeared, I seized it! I started planning in-class flips with my seventh graders. Little was available on the how-to of this type of flip at the time, so it became a trial-and-error teaching process. Similarly, Carolina was trying to innovate in her classrooms. Flipping had already become part of her DNA, so she decided to embrace this new technique in her online class. She used the breakout room feature in Blackboard Collaborate to have students in different groups access content and perform various tasks. Then, she took this model to her face-to-face English course to teach writing mechanics and punctuation.

In our different teaching settings, we encountered new ways to use the in-class flip, whether it was face-to-face or online, and in doing so, our understanding of the in-class flip started taking different shapes and evolving in our own planning. We started sharing our work, which led to getting to know other teachers using the same approach. Teachers around the world told us how they did the in-class flip, and we discovered a myriad of options. To begin with, we found the following:

- The teaching configurations could vary according to different needs and lesson objectives.

- You can design an in-class flip in the form of stations or as a class moment.

- Planning decisions depend on specific topics or lessons.

- Students can access the flipped content in different ways. These ways do not necessarily imply station work or technology use.

- It is possible to put the in-class flip in place successfully, regardless of available resources or content options.

With this in mind, we have defined the in-class flip thus:

> **IN-CLASS FLIP:** *A set of adaptable in-class configurations where individual and group spaces coexist, allowing flipped learning to take place within the educational setting.*

Blended, Flipped, or In-Class Flip?

After applying blended learning methodologies for years in different contexts, we could not ignore our knowledge of this topic. After all, it was our interest in blended learning that led us to discover flipped learning. Along the way, we encountered an important question, which has to do with the role of blended learning within a flipped learning environment. We analyzed what different experts from the field of blended learning have presented regarding the in-class flip. Table 1.1 presents a brief description of those who have directly invoked the term "in-class flip," or who refer to its basic underlying principles.

After analyzing these philosophies regarding the in-class flip, there were some aspects that needed clarification. For us, videos are one way of offering content, but as you will see later, they are not absolutely necessary. Therefore, our model of the in-class flip is not necessarily a blended learning subset. Additionally, we move beyond station rotation in our configurations. Technology for us is optional (as it is for many teachers in Colombia and other countries). We don't always have access to technology in all our classrooms, but we still apply the in-class flip successfully and in various ways.

On the other hand, Horn, Staker, and Tucker discuss flipped learning as if it were interchangeable with blended learning—which, for us, is not necessarily the case.

TABLE 1.1

Approaches to Flipped Learning That Reference the In-Class Flip

SOURCE AND AUTHOR	REFERENCE
Michael Horn and Heather Staker *Blended: Using Disruptive Innovation to Improve Schools* (2014)	Horn and Staker present a blended learning rotation model. It contains four sub-models. One of the sub-models is called the station rotation. It is similar to an in-class flip, with its online instruction, station rotation, and collaborative activities. However, the model includes teacher-led instruction, which is not a teaching aim of flipped learning.
Caitlin Tucker Blog: caitlintucker.com	Tucker blogs about how she combines station rotation with flipped learning. She mentions pre-recorded lectures within the stations.
Caitlin Tucker, Tiffany Wycoff, and Jason T. Green *Blended Learning in Action: A Practical Guide Toward Sustainable Change* (2017)	Tucker et al. talk about the Whole Group Rotation and the Free Station Rotation. For her (and for Gonzalez), one of the stations always involves a computer or devices for students to watch videos in class.
Mark Barnes and Jennifer Gonzalez *Hacking Education: 10 Quick Fixes for Every School* (2015)	Barnes and Gonzalez describe the in-class flip within a station rotation model. For them, the in-class flip is "a subset of blended learning . . . making it fall under the blended learning umbrella" (p. 93). This means it requires the use of technology.

A few years ago, if you were a traditional teacher and wanted to spice things up, you would add an online component to your class and, voila, you had a blended classroom. But with flipped learning, you have to undergo a mindset shift in order for it to work. You need to become a "Professional Educator" (Flipped Learning Network, 2014) and challenge yourself to collaborate with others and share your practice. You need to transform the environment in your class into a flexible one, playing around with the arrangement of chairs and tables and access to resources. With flipped learning, your mind has to change, not just the place where you put your materials.

Jon Bergmann describes flipped learning as "the meta-strategy that allows all other strategies to work," including the in-class flip. We didn't discover the in-class flip while implementing blended learning; it happened when we had already flipped our classes. So, is the in-class flip blended learning or flipped learning? We see it as a form of flipped learning, since it adheres to the essential principles of the flipped approach: direct instruction is not given by the teacher in front of the classroom but via other means (video, textbook, PowerPoint slides, etc.). This change leads to a transformation of the group learning space. It turns into a dynamic environment where students engage creatively with the subject matter. If teachers have computers at their disposal and want to incorporate technology as part of the mix, they can. In that sense, the in-class flip can be considered blended learning, but technology is not a requirement. The in-class flip stands on its own as a way to flip your classroom when the traditional flip doesn't work.

We had many hits and misses when experimenting with different ways to do in-class flips in various teaching contexts. Along the way we discovered that the in-class flip could be set up with a variety of adaptable configurations. We identified two main types of in-class flip: station and in situ (non-station). We also identified six different types of stations that allowed flexibility when implementing the configurations. In the next section, we will describe each one of them, and you can decide which would be most appropriate for your context and your students. Are you ready to rethink instruction?

TEACHING SPOTLIGHT

Dr. Gwo-Jen Hwang is a chair professor at the National Taiwan University of Science and Technology in Taiwan. He shared his story about using the in-class flip strategy in Taiwan's rural schools. In these rural areas, technology access is unavailable in students' homes, so schools have decided to do an in-school flip. It is called an in-school flip because it is not focused on one teacher's initiative in a specific classroom setting. Instead, it is a school-wide initiative.

In Taiwanese schools, students come one hour early to clean and do service. Now they come an additional hour earlier to access the computer classroom. At school each student sits at a computer to access the materials before class. This is done on the school grounds, so families don't need to worry about getting computers or about an internet connection. In Taiwan, most parents whose children attend rural schools work long hours, so having kids at school for more of the day actually helps them.

Dr. Hwang says that in-class flipping has been a great way to give parents peace and tranquility about their children. The school provides all the necessary access to information and materials; parents are not expected to invest money on additional technology.

Types of the In-Class Flip

Do you like what you hear, but you can't yet envision it happening in your classroom? You might choose a different type of in-class flip, depending on your mode of teaching, the ages of your students, or the setting where you teach. Choosing a specific configuration will also depend on the amount of information you have to provide, the type of students you have, or the type of resources you have access to. You can use the decision tree in Figure 1.1 to help you reach those decisions as well as to support the information you will read in the coming sections.

Station Work

Station rotation is not new, and neither is flipped learning. What is new, however, is how these two come together in the group learning space to provide better learning opportunities and different teaching approaches. Even though many educators have turned to stations for years as a way to make learning more active in their classrooms, the way in which we have used stations in in-class flips differs in several ways:

1. It can be done with or without technology (Ramirez, 2018).

2. Stations always aim at developing one of Bloom's thinking skills.

3. We have tweaked the existing offer of stations so that they fit a flipped learning environment.

4. Stations consider the four pillars of flipped learning.

We have found different rotation strategies within the in-class flip station model. We have classified them as *sequenced*, *looped*, *mixed*, and *half 'n' half*. Each configuration supports different purposes, and you can adapt each one in many ways to accommodate every teacher's individual context. Read more about how these configurations work in Chapter 5.

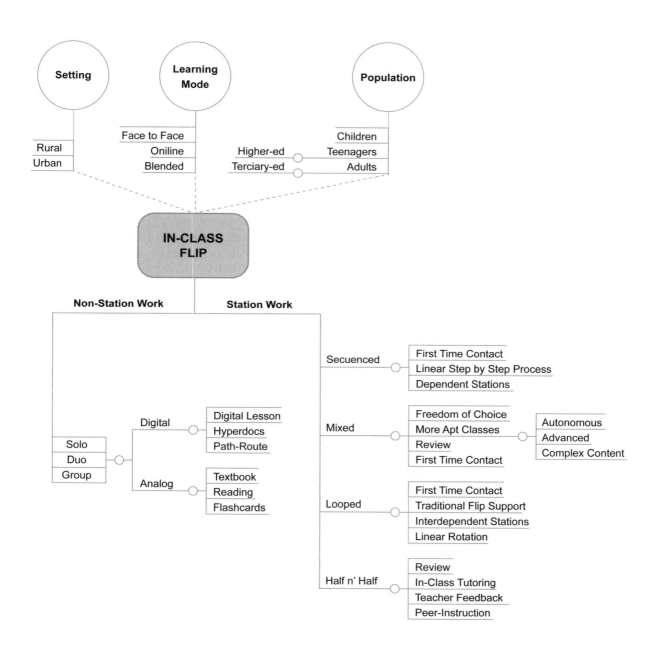

Figure 1.1. Decision tree. What type of in-class flip should I use?

In-Situ (Non-Station) Work

We have found an alternative to station work. Students can access flipped content within the teaching setting (where they share a learning space with the teacher) on their own (solo flip), working with a partner (duo flip), or through group work (group flip).

The in-class flip offers direct instruction via alternative materials within the group learning space, so in-situ work can be done in many ways according to student interaction. With the solo, duo, and group in-class flip, the teacher is no longer delivering instruction at the center of the class. These become favorable alternatives when students come to class without having prepared the flipped content (as in a regular out-of-class flip).

You can construct in-situ work in different ways to ensure that students access information and engage with the content and activities. Keep in mind that even though students are doing "the same thing" and doing it at their own pace, you remain simply a guide on the side. Are you ready to let go of control? It sounds scary, we know. But relinquishing control and handing it over to our students has been one of the best actions we have taken as teachers. We want you to discover the many benefits of putting your students in the driver's seat of their own learning process. Read more about in-situ work in Chapter 3.

REFLECTIVE PAUSE

What are some reasons you and your school might implement the in-class flip? Would you choose the in-class method over the original flipped learning method, or would you mix them?

THE IN-CLASS FLIP AROUND THE WORLD

"My lower-level students wouldn't complete any work outside of the class. The in-class flip was my way of eliminating homework and still being able to individually help students."—Rebekah Cerqua, chemistry teacher, Greenfield, USA

CHAPTER 2

Twenty Reasons to Consider the In-Class Flip

> **This chapter addresses several ISTE Standards:**
>
> **2.1. Learner**
> Educators continually improve their practice by learning from and with others and exploring proven and promising practices that leverage technology to improve student learning. Educators:
>
> a. *Set professional learning goals to explore and apply pedagogical approaches made possible by technology and reflect on their effectiveness.*
>
> c. *Stay current with research that supports improved student learning outcomes, including findings from the learning sciences.*
>
> **2.2. Leader**
> Educators seek out opportunities for leadership to support student empowerment and success and to improve teaching and learning. Educators:
>
> b. *Advocate for equitable access to educational technology, digital content, and learning opportunities to meet the diverse needs of all students.*

THERE ARE MANY REASONS WHY THE IN-CLASS FLIP COULD BENEFIT both you and your students. We have continued exploring it over the years and uncovering its layers to the point that we built the ability to write this book. Are you interested in our twenty reasons for trying the in-class flip? Keep reading!

Naturally, many of the following reasons also apply to traditional flipping; however, in-class flipping also offers specific benefits that are not possible in a traditional flip.

Reason 1: The in-class flip addresses challenges

Many teachers have tried flipping their classes without success. This is primarily due to a lack of student compliance. Students are a) not doing the individual work that comes with accessing flipped content, b) coming to class unprepared to show what they learned on their own, c) facing a lack of resources to work with at home, and/or d) beholden to strict homework policies. All of these challenges hinder the teacher's ability to shape traditional flip work effectively.

Reason 2: Student-centered classes

In an in-class flip, the spotlight traditionally placed on the teacher inevitably shifts to the student. The teacher becomes the "guide on the side" by providing meaningful learning opportunities and facilitating learning.

Reason 3: Student autonomy

Planning an in-class flip involves thinking of active learning and decision-making opportunities that allow students to be accountable for their learning, leading to student autonomy. Even though the teacher is readily available, students learn to access content on their own.

Reason 4: Improved student focus

When we plan activities with a high level of responsibility placed on each student, with a clear outcome, and with the flipped content at their fingertips, the opportunity for distractions is minimized.

Reason 5: Increased content coverage

In an in-class flip, many activities can be condensed, and time seems to stretch within a class period. This effect is most evident in a station work setting. We estimate that a three-hour lesson could be completed in one hour using station rotation. Your results may vary, but we think you'll quickly see what we mean.

Reason 6: Recognition of student individuality

Thanks to the micro-conversations you can have with every student, you will get to know each of them better and respond better as a teacher and as a person. In-class flipping definitely helps you treat each student as an individual.

Reason 7: Immediate and personalized feedback

Less teacher talking time and more student learning time allows more teacher feedback time. As students are learning the content in class, the teacher is walking around and stepping in when needed. This assistance does not occur when students are accessing the content on their own, with no teacher available.

In a regular flipped class, unless the teacher is synchronously available when flipping takes place outside the teaching setting, answers to student questions must be provided later. Sometimes students struggle with the content and need to clarify a doubt right away to continue learning. In an in-class flip, the teacher is right there, ready to respond to any questions or doubts.

Reason 8: Flip the "unflippable"

Some content is considered "unflippable" because of its level of complexity. In-class flipping allows the teacher to guide the process without requiring students to tackle complex content independently. Students can feel secure because the teacher is right there to assist when necessary.

Reason 9: No homework, no problem

The in-class flip has become a powerful response to "no homework" policy advocates. You'll also be sure students are doing their own work and not having someone else do it for them. Thanks to the flipped content accessed in class, homework is no longer an issue.

Reason 10: Control your resources

One reason flipped learning may fall apart is that some students lack the necessary resources to access content outside of school. In an in-class flip setting, teachers become technology managers and content designers, so they can structure the learning experience with what they have at hand. Thus, teachers are in control of what resources they use, and do not have to depend on what students can access at home.

Reason 11: Get hooked!

Students love in-class flips! They can fast forward, pause, and rewind, as well as ask questions. When they have an active role in their own learning, students get hooked, and teachers get hooked too!

Reason 12: Support young learners

Two characteristics that distinguish young learners from older ones are their low level of autonomy and short attention span. Naturally, they are at the beginning of their learning process and need guidance in becoming independent learners. While this happens, assigning a traditional flipped task could be counterproductive; parents or caregivers are generally not trained to provide the help the child needs. In-class flipping allows the teacher to guide young learners and be present while they access flipped content, without depending on at-home support, which is, unfortunately, not always available.

Reason 13: Offer choice

Let's say you have students at different levels of mastery. In an in-class flip, students can be given a choice to decide what to learn according to their needs. That way, advanced students are not expected to review what they already know, and struggling students can take the time they need to fully understand a topic.

Reason 14: Help out your substitute teacher

As a substitute, have you ever had a class where you had to teach a lesson you had never taught, or one that you hadn't reviewed in years? With an in-class flip, the substitute teacher can avoid the dread of teaching content he or she is not familiar with. The substitute can easily provide a meaningful class experience without being a subject expert.

Reason 15: A more active role for special education aides

Though it is not the case in all educational settings, some classrooms count on teaching aides to support specific learner needs. With an in-class flip lesson, the teacher can focus on supporting students by using more active learning tasks, thanks to the flipped explanations already provided. At the same time, teaching aides could benefit from the flipped content to enhance their role and their own understanding of students' needs by supporting students more closely. Since the content is readily available in the classroom context, the aid has direct access to the information and can guide the learning of the student as well as count on the head teacher's support while the class is working autonomously..

Reason 16: More 1:1 teacher–student talking time

One of the most rewarding benefits of flipping inside and outside of class is having more individual interactions with students and getting to know them better. Teacher talking time is reduced, allowing meaningful 1:1 teacher–student talking time to increase.

Reason 17: Becoming *that* teacher

Since the teacher is available to speak to different students individually, he/she gets to know them better. Thus, stronger student-teacher relationships exist. The in-class flip facilitates being *that* teacher who notices and acts when something is wrong.

Reason 18: Less opportunity for cheating

Students cheat for multiple reasons, including laziness, lack of time to do the task, or lack of understanding. Whatever the reason, the in-class flip makes it harder to cheat, because the content is being accessed in class. There is less space for laziness, lack of time, or student miscomprehension because the teacher is around to provide support and ensure students are doing what they are supposed to do.

Reason 19: Differentiation

Thanks to the flexibility that in-class flip configurations offer and the time that opens up in our teaching schedule, we can design lessons that cater to all students' needs differently within the same setting.

Reason 20: Growth

Given the reasons above, with the in-class flip, growth takes place in many ways. The teacher grows as a professional educator, inevitably reflecting on and rethinking their teaching practice thanks to the possibility to observe closely and interact with students and their learning in various ways. Likewise, students continue growing as individuals and as learners, developing their autonomy and receiving the support they need. The relationships among teachers and students also grow through one-to-one conversations and more personalized feedback and assistance.

Have these twenty reasons convinced you? Whether you are already flipping, are looking for a way to relinquish control, or have encountered setbacks in traditional flipping, we invite you to give the in-class flip a try. It is a great solution to many of the constraints you may have in your teaching context.

TEACHING SPOTLIGHT

Heath Chittenden is the principal of Ashhurst School, the first fully flipped school in New Zealand. In 2012, Heath heard about the flipped classroom and decided to start flipping reading.

Heath wanted a school where students had autonomy over their learning and where the teachers could position themselves in a way that they could enhance student learning. Even though there was an integration of technology (Google and YouTube in most classes), Heath wanted to go the extra mile. Ashhurst cares about "the activation of knowledge and engagement with it students can achieve." Therefore, teachers are considered "activators of learning." For Heath, the mere engagement of students in activities is not enough. He says that "as the flip model changes the relationship between teachers and students, the activation of knowledge is their main concern."

Ashhurst's teachers generate learning experiences where students are always at the center, using different configurations of the in-class flip to guarantee the engagement of students with content at many different levels. To learn more about what Ashhurst does, go to www.ashhurst.school.nz.

REFLECTIVE PAUSE

What is your reason for in-class flipping? Do you still have hesitations?

THE IN-CLASS FLIP AROUND THE WORLD

"I used to do the at-home-flip, and one day I had my students start their homework early in class. It was so much better to have kids watching the video in class so that I was there to help answer questions and everyone had access to technology."
—Kyle Niemis, seventh-grade science teacher, South Brunswick, New Jersey, USA

CHAPTER 3

In-Situ Work

> **This chapter addresses several ISTE Standards:**
>
> ### 2.3. Citizen
> Educators inspire students to positively contribute to and responsibly partici-
> pate in the digital world. Educators:
>
> a. *Create experiences for learners to make positive, socially responsible contri-
> butions and exhibit empathetic behavior online that build relationships and
> community.*
>
> b. *Establish a learning culture that promotes curiosity and critical examination of
> online resources and fosters digital literacy and media fluency.*
>
> ### 2.5. Designer
> Educators design authentic, learner-driven activities and environments that
> recognize and accommodate learner variability. Educators:

a. Use technology to create, adapt, and personalize learning experiences that foster independent learning and accommodate learner differences and needs.

b. Design authentic learning activities that align with content area standards and use digital tools and resources to maximize active, deep learning.

c. Explore and apply instructional design principles to create innovative digital learning environments that engage and support learning.

2.6. Facilitator

Educators facilitate learning with technology to support student achievement of the ISTE Standards for Students. Educators:

a. Foster a culture where students take ownership of their learning goals and outcomes in both independent and group settings.

c. Create learning opportunities that challenge students to use a design process and computational thinking to innovate and solve problems.

d. Model and nurture creativity and creative expression to communicate ideas, knowledge or connections.

PRIOR TO 2020, THE IDEA OF AN IN-SITU IN-CLASS FLIP (without stations) might not have been clear or even necessary for people teaching face-to-face. It may have been interpreted as a complex name for a digital lesson. However, today, after flipping our classes in a digital setting, we can put our fingers on specific practices and actions that clarify the purpose and advantages of this type of in-class flip.

First of all, location is an important aspect to clarify about the in-situ in-class flip. We can carry out an in-situ in-class flip in a physical or digital classroom. However, regardless of the location where the lesson will take place, we need a digital hub to host it. This space might be a digital lesson, a HyperDoc, or a SOFLA® lesson, among others. Having a well-crafted digital "one-stop shop" is crucial to ensure students' understanding, autonomy, and engagement with the content and each other at the right moment within the lesson.

We define the in-class flip as "the coexistence of the individual and group learning spaces within the same classroom setting." We can have a class where the direct instruction is not given by the teacher at the front of the classroom, but through different means such as videos, readings, and infographics, among others. When this happens, we affirm we are delivering an in-situ in-class flip because we are not the ones teaching the content directly at the front of the classroom; rather, students are accessing it on their own. The elements of this configuration are: content delivered through alternative means and accessed by students independently, multiple means of interaction (students and content, students among themselves, and students and the teacher), collaboration, and the many roles participants can play.

In an in-situ in-class flip, interaction and collaboration are crucial. The point of not having a regular lesson where the teacher teaches and the students learn is to generate deeper learning and to guarantee that students engage with the content and with each other better, creating a true student-centered atmosphere. In the pursuit of this student-centeredness, teachers promote collaboration and interaction within the in-class flip through engaging activities, well-thought-out designs, and active learning strategies, ensuring the development of digital-age skills.

Also, in an in-situ in-class flip, teacher decision-making acts as a catalyst in the generation of optimal learning experiences for students (just as with the out-of-class flip). Teachers' decision-making guides the learning path, transforming a dull teacher-fronted lesson into a dynamic experience where students become autonomous agents of their own learning process. It might sound contradictory to say that teachers' decisions drive students' autonomy, but we have corroborated that teachers' decisions regarding tasks and student choice ensure students' engagement with their own learning process, resulting in learner empowerment.

Thus, an in-situ in-class flip considers the importance of student engagement, involvement at different levels, the need for specific activities that place students at the center of the learning process, and the availability of content offered through different means to cater to all students in the class. Furthermore, deciding to flip content in this way gives teachers more time to focus on students, while the flipped content is presented in a more concrete way. What we mean to say is that when we have selected or designed material and use that material in class, instead of providing the direct instruction ourselves, we have noticed that time is used more consciously for learning (e.g., twenty minutes of direct instruction might be reduced to a five-minute video, leaving ample time for practice and authentic student engagement).

As opposed to station work (see Chapter 5), you can plan this type of flip for every class, since to plan it, you can start with your regular lesson plan and simply insert the content to be accessed within the lesson through alternative media. This type of lesson does not ask you to visualize rotations, but rather invites you to build a self-paced learning experience for students. And, because you are not delivering direct instruction, you become more available to focus on individual students and their needs.

Even though the in-situ in-class flip consists of a sequential lesson, and students interact with this content inside of the classroom (not outside, as in the "out-of-class flip"), they can do so individually (the solo in-situ in-class flip); in pairs (the duo in-situ in-class flip); and in groups (the group in-situ in-class flip). The patterns of interaction of the students with the content can be decided by the teacher when planning, or by the students when accessing the lesson. In this sense, the students have the opportunity to develop the different levels of Bloom's taxonomy within a lesson. The next section examines some of the elements that should be considered to make the in-situ in-class flip configuration effective.

Delivering Flipped Content

In the out-of-class flip, where students are expected to do homework on their own time and to come to class prepared for the lesson, in an in-situ in-class flip, students are provided with content that replaces the direct instruction given in the classroom— this is a major (if not the main) difference between an in-situ in-class flip and other types of lessons. In this section, we provide an overview of different ways to present content to students using this methodology. For a more detailed, step-by-step process on how to plan in-class flip content, we invite you to explore Chapter 8.

Video in Real Time with Accountability

As in the traditional flip, video is a very effective way to deliver instruction if it's approached well. You might want to deliver instruction via videos within an in-class flip for many reasons, including ease of access, students' existing familiarity with the technology (i.e., video platforms), and ease of elaboration (some teachers are already expert video makers), among others. Thus, you might offer video as the first part of your in-situ in-class flip lesson. As many authors suggest, videos alone do not necessarily help learning, so we suggest adding some form of accountability to the watching of a video (Bergmann & Sams, 2012; Musallam, 2013; Kirsch, 2014). Students must engage with the content from the start of the video to the end to make the best out of it. Inserting questions, tasks, or reflection prompts will enrich the viewing experience.

Reading in Real Time with Accountability

For centuries, students have learned through reading. For that reason, reading is also a privileged learning strategy in an in-situ in-class flip. Teachers can ask students to read a text individually within the class time and later ask questions and promote discussion about it. However, to make this experience more suited to digital-age needs, teachers can use social reading platforms (Mazur, 2020) to engage students even further with questions, comments, and discussion in real time (synchronously). This practice can optimize the use of time, classmates, and the teacher, while at the same time optimizing the use of reading as a learning tool.

Visual Content Analysis

Visual learning experts suggest that there is a positive impact of images on students' understanding of concepts and topics. According to Weinstein et al. (2018, p. 112), "pictures are generally remembered better than words, and can provide an additional memory cue." With this in mind, some of the flipped content we design contains strong visual elements (e.g., sketchnotes and infographics).

Using Sketchnotes Sketchnotes are a very powerful tool for explaining topics to students, since they are packed with information within only one frame. This tool invites students to do exhaustive analyses and to think strategically in trying to understand a topic from images. Fernandez-Fontecha et al. define sketchnotes as a means to communicate abstract ideas multi-modally through a myriad of resources (e.g., linguistic, graphic, drawings, etc.) that result in a concrete "depiction of abstract concepts and ideas for a non-specialist audience" (2018, p. 1). Thus, the teacher can synthesize a large amount of information in one visual note while fostering higher-order thinking skills. Figure 3.1 shows an example of a sketchnote used in an in-situ group in-class flip.

Using Infographics Much like sketchnotes, infographics provide a visual representation of data and information in a quick and concise way. The main differences between the two are that infographics are digital (using icons or images instead of drawings), and they are ideal when showing statistics, patterns, and trends. Using an infographic for flipped content not only saves time and lowers students' cognitive load (avoiding overwhelming them with too much information), it also develops students' interpretative skills (California Academy of Sciences, n.d.).

Choice Boards

Another interesting way to deliver content to students is through choice boards. According to CAST (2018, para. 1), one of the principles of Universal Design for Learning is "to provide multiple means of representation" in order to respond to students' variances and needs. In its guidelines for the first principle, CAST (2018) suggests providing content in ways that do not depend on only one sense (hearing, sight, touch, etc.). When thinking of ways to present content to students through different means, choice boards provide an interesting way to offer content multi-modally. The teacher can prepare a choice board with the same information using different means: textual, oral, or visual, in order to respond to the varied needs in the classroom. Additionally, teachers can ensure accessibility by using multiple technologies (closed captions, immersive readers, etc.) within the choice board. It goes without saying that students develop autonomy and agency when learning from a choice board since they need to decide for themselves the best way to learn.

Learning Menus

A learning menu operates very similarly to a choice board, but it differs in design. Teachers can create learning menus to present content to students and to promote agency and autonomy. Sometimes, we teachers feel we have to teach every concept and idea in our syllabus, but this practice might not be in sync with students' interests and preferences. If we create a learning menu offering what we think they need to learn, but give it to them to decide what to pursue, we will have better-engaged learners learning what resonates with them and what adapts to their learning objectives.

Games with Flipped Content

Games as a tool for learning are as old as the hills. In education they are commonly used to practice or apply a concept. They can also be a fantastic tool for teaching content to students in a fun and dynamic way. Adding flipped content within a game is a good way to offer in-class flip material. Teachers can design games to teach content, or, even better, have students design their own games. Students can learn from cards, board games, strategy games, dice, and cubes, among others. And nowadays, all of these game types can be easily designed digitally.

Using Flipped Instructions

During the COVID-19 pandemic, one of the biggest lessons learned was the need to provide accessible instructions to students. As students presented different types of connection issues during their virtual classes, we saw ourselves repeating instructions over and over, whether it was because students had lost their internet connection, had problems with their audio, or had connected late to class. It became imperative to design instructions in a way that would avoid repetition on the teacher's part and allow continuous access to what was being done in class at any time it was required. Martha came up with what she called "flipped differentiated instructions," combining Bondie and Zusho's (2018) Inclusive Directions with flipped learning. This required presenting instructions to students in a variety of ways (written, audio, video) and specifying time, steps, language use, roles, rules, turn-taking, and task (Ramírez, 2021).

Creating Digital Learning Paths

One way in which we have designed flipped content is through what we have termed "digital learning paths": we provide a path or route that students must follow to get from point A to point B. We called them paths because students have to follow specific steps to complete the lesson; they cannot skip any steps. In some cases, the lesson might look like an actual path because of the digital tool used in its design. The lessons are linear, yet some might include choices on how to complete them. Moreover, they can be used in virtual or face-to-face settings. So far, we have identified four types of paths:

Decision-making paths: This type of lesson allows students to take ownership of their learning because they are given choices regarding what content or type of task they want to focus on to complete a lesson. This gives students freedom, even though the lesson has a specific route that must be followed. For example, if a student is learning about a specific topic and needs to be able to apply it by the end of the lesson, the teacher might provide choices on how to learn the content by offering the flipped explanation in different learning modes for them to choose from (video, podcast, website, etc.) or they could be offered a choice in how they present what they have learned.

Escape rooms: An escape room is a type of challenge in which players (in this case students) "are locked in a room and have to search for clues, work together, and solve puzzles to escape" (Lyman, 2021, p. ix). Here, the flipped content is presented within the "escape room" format. Students must cover the content and complete some type of task or challenge to unlock the room. This activity can be done digitally or in a face-to-face classroom setting.

Didactic sequence: Instructional design models insist on the importance of defining steps and tasks for students to successfully navigate a learning unit or topic autonomously. In this type of sequence, the teacher makes the decisions and places them transparently in the lesson design, signaling the steps students have to follow. In this sequence, content and tasks are embedded for students to access on their own.

HyperDocs: Lisa Highfill, Kelly Hilton, and Sarah Landis (2016, p. 72) proposed the term HyperDocs to "describe the digital lesson design and delivery of instruction that was happening in (their) classrooms." Instead of writing lesson plans for themselves, they crafted online lessons for their students with the help of Google tools and apps. HyperDocs (HyperDocs.co) became a solution for teachers looking to engage their students further in their learning with the help of the Google Suite and some instructional design principles.

TEACHING SPOTLIGHT

Kate Baker is a high school English teacher in Manahawkin, New Jersey. She has deployed BYOD and #flipclass methods to inspire her students to think critically and become passionate about the topics studied in class. She blends modern and classical elements in the study of literature.

Kate had a brilliant idea. She uses one of the most organized in-class flip structures we have seen. For Kate, having eighth and ninth graders moving around became a nightmare, so instead of having students rotate, her stations rotate. She organizes her students in groups and gives them an agenda with all the different tasks they need to complete and the times for each one. She also gives them a digital lesson designed in GoFormative. In the lesson, students do tasks and show accountability for their work in real time. Kate's attention to detail is amazing, making the learning experience worthwhile and easy for every learner in her class.

REFLECTIVE PAUSE

- Have you used any of these in-situ (non-station) configurations before?
- Can you think of teaching moments where a solo, duo, or group flip might replace direct instruction in your classes?

THE IN-CLASS FLIP AROUND THE WORLD

"My system is always the same in my flipped mastery classroom. I have students complete each unit through the use of a HyperDoc to guide the order of tasks they complete. The general arrangement is video/Google Slides for note taking, followed by an open note quiz for students to check their note taking and preliminary understanding. Whenever a quiz is not mastered, they must remediate and retake the quiz. Students will go through several of these cycles in the HyperDoc. After these are finished, students complete a standards review that asks questions geared to specific standards. This is the students' last check before attempting the mastery quiz. Once this quiz has been mastered, students are qualified to take the test for the unit."

—Jake Habegger, American history teacher, Franklin, Tennessee, USA

CHAPTER 4

The Station Setup Space

This chapter addresses several ISTE Standards:

2.5. Designer

Educators design authentic, learner-driven activities and environments that recognize and accommodate learner variability. Educators:

b. Design authentic learning activities that align with content area standards and use digital tools and resources to maximize active, deep learning.

c. Explore and apply instructional design principles to create innovative digital learning environments that engage and support learning.

2.6. Facilitator

Educators facilitate learning with technology to support student achievement of the ISTE Standards for Students. Educators:

a. Foster a culture where students take ownership of their learning goals and outcomes in both independent and group settings.

c. Create learning opportunities that challenge students to use a design process and computational thinking to innovate and solve problems.

BEFORE WE REVIEW THE PLANNING OF DIFFERENT STATION TYPES, let's clarify what we mean by "stations." The way stations are organized depends on many factors:

- The classroom or learning space(s)
- The number of students
- The types of teaching resources
- The available classroom furniture (e.g., desks, tables, puffs, chairs, etc.)

Classroom Preparation for the In-Class Flip

Every classroom and every context is different. It is important for you to locate a specific area within the learning space to set up each station. You can do this by assigning a station to a specific table, a classroom corner, or a set of desks, or even by marking

Figure 4.1. Different types of station setups.

the floor with tape to identify the designated space for these stations. Tables, chairs, and desks are not necessary for a station to work; you can use the walls and floor space to display material for students to work with. You can even place stations in different classrooms if available (or necessary).

The four types of setups can adapt to different contexts, classroom settings, and learning possibilities (as shown in Figure 4.1). Imagine the myriad of activities that can be done in each station.

TEACHING SPOTLIGHT

Alexa Finck is a high school Spanish teacher in Seattle, Washington. She has included Virtual Reality (VR) in her Spanish classes as a strategy to make language learning more meaningful and authentic. In one lesson, she used an in-class flip to review commands using five stations.

1. Stop game: Students took command cards out of a bag and completed a chart as fast as possible.

2. Jenga game: Students played with some commands on slips of paper.

3. A song listening task to identify the commands: Students provided their insights on the story of the song based on familiar vocabulary and structures they found in it.

4. A teacher support station to clarify doubts.

5. A VR game called "Keep Talking and Nobody Explodes." The mission is to deactivate a bomb. In this station, the student leader wore the VR headset and could see the bomb; the team had the deactivation manual but depended on the leader's descriptions. Based on the descriptions, the team checked the manual and provided commands for the leader to complete the mission.

In Alexa's words, "Students could understand the value and importance of clear commands through the game, which they had not been able to grasp completely through the station work. Having the ability to see authentic application of the language made it meaningful. Through VR, they were able to make that 'click' of what they are learning with reality."

Types of Stations

The in-class configurations (explained in Chapter 5) become adaptable through seven types of stations: flip, practice, independent, teacher support, peer instruction, assessment, and feedback. These will serve different learning purposes and provide flexibility within the station configurations. Nevertheless, in a station in-class flip, the flip station is essential for flipped learning to take place within each configuration. Let's review what each station is intended for.

Flip Station

In this type of station, you offer the flipped content. This station replaces the teacher's direct instruction through a variety of means, such as video, slides, flashcards, online sources, reading material, HyperDocs, student-made material, podcasts, etc.

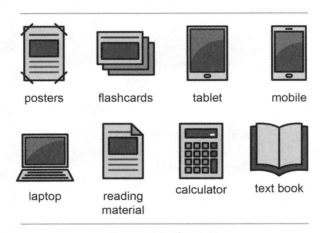

Figure 4.2. Flip station.

Practice Station

Through practice stations, learners are asked to show mastery of the flipped content. The activities in this station will depend on two aspects: the aims set for the lesson and the level of difficulty students can handle. Practice stations should take students through all the levels of Bloom's taxonomy. They should also be scaffolded. Practice activities may include worksheets, online tasks, games, discussions, speaking activities, pair work, group creation, writing, experiments, arts and crafts, videos, recordings, role-plays, and more. The key to any activity in this type of station is to encourage active learning. The sky and your creativity are the limit!

For an in-class flip to occur, there should be flip stations and practice stations. If there is no flipped content available, then the teacher would be doing the station work via direct instruction.

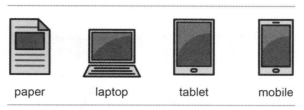

Figure 4.3. Practice station.

Independent Station

The number of students, their work pace, and the types of activities offered may sometimes require an extra station that allows a smoother rotation. For instance, some students might finish before the next station is available, leading to a "student traffic jam." For this situation, the independent station becomes a valuable option that allows students to continue learning instead of waiting and wasting precious time.

An independent station is a type of "learning waiting room"—ideal for students to work in until the flip or practice stations become available. The type of activity planned in this station should be one that any student can work on that is not directly linked to the flipped content of the current station work. That is to say, it should be an activity about content students already know. Teachers can plan reviews, hands-on activities, games, crafts, worksheets, online activities, or silent reading, for the independent station.

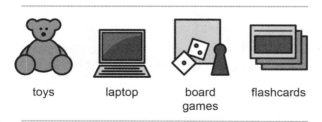

Figure 4.4. Independent station.

Teacher Support Station

This is a station where the teacher plays an important role in working with students to clarify questions, tutor them, or provide feedback. Sometimes, providing content in the flip station is not enough. Some topics require more teacher intervention and further scaffolding. In such circumstances, you can place the teacher support station either as one of the points along the path, or as an "outside station" where students get direct instruction and assistance from the teacher. Other times, this station might be used as a feedback space, where students can get one-on-one time with the teacher to revise an assignment or ask questions about their personal learning process.

Figure 4.5. Teacher support station.

Peer-Instruction Station

Harvard professor Eric Mazur popularized peer instruction in 1997. In his physics class, he proposed that his students explain their answers and convince each other that their choice was correct. He claims that because students share cognitive levels, they can be more effective in explaining the material to one another, since they don't have the "expert blind spot" (Wiggins & McTighe, 2006) that sometimes prevents educators from giving information to students in the clearest possible way.

Inspired by Mazur's technique, we found great value in allowing students to learn from each other. We include a peer-instruction station for students to teach each other as a way to show mastery of the content. In a peer-instruction station, you can provide small whiteboards and markers, or paper and pens, and ask students to teach the content to each other. You can establish your own ground rules for the peer-instruction station. How should students teach the concepts? How should they decide who teaches and who learns? How should they use their notes to craft the peer-instruction? How are they held accountable for what they are learning or teaching?

Figure 4.6. Peer-instruction station.

Feedback Station

We include a station dedicated to providing feedback, which can vary according to the lesson. The main uses we have found are shared in Table 4.1.

TABLE 4.1
Feedback Station

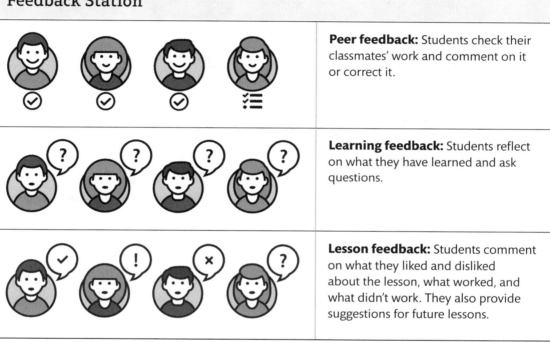

	Peer feedback: Students check their classmates' work and comment on it or correct it.
	Learning feedback: Students reflect on what they have learned and ask questions.
	Lesson feedback: Students comment on what they liked and disliked about the lesson, what worked, and what didn't work. They also provide suggestions for future lessons.

You can collect feedback using online tools, post-its, worksheets, video, or written tasks. You should include student feedback in your planning and decide on your expectations about it.

Assessment Station

In this station, students do a specific task to show their level of mastery. This task can be a quiz, a test, or an activity that requires cumulative knowledge of the content learned to complete it. The tasks at this station can be graded at the teacher's discretion.

Figure 4.6. Assessment station.

Conclusion

Each station will play an important role in the learning experience, depending on the configuration you use. We predict you will create your own types of stations, since every context is unique. After all, in the words of Jon Bergmann, "Flipped learning is not static. It is evolving because of research, class innovation, and technology" (FL Worldwide LLC, 2022).

5

Station Rotation Configurations

> **This chapter addresses several ISTE Standards:**
>
> **2.1. Learner**
> Educators continually improve their practice by learning from and with others and exploring proven and promising practices that leverage technology to improve student learning. Educators:
>
> c. *Stay current with research that supports improved student learning outcomes, including findings from the learning sciences.*
>
> **2.5. Designer**
> Educators design authentic, learner-driven activities and environments that recognize and accommodate learner variability. Educators:
>
> a. *Use technology to create, adapt, and personalize learning experiences that foster independent learning and accommodate learner differences and needs.*
>
> b. *Design authentic learning activities that align with content area standards and use digital tools and resources to maximize active, deep learning.*

> c. Explore and apply instructional design principles to create innovative digital learning environments that engage and support learning.
>
> ### 2.6. Facilitator
> Educators facilitate learning with technology to support student achievement of the ISTE Standards for Students. Educators:
>
> a. Foster a culture where students take ownership of their learning goals and outcomes in both independent and group settings.
>
> c. Create learning opportunities that challenge students to use a design process and computational thinking to innovate and solve problems.

THIS CHAPTER FEATURES THE DIFFERENT TYPES OF CONFIGURATIONS, which include sequenced, looped, mixed, and half 'n' half. The chapter figures illustrate the setup for each configuration, followed by a description of how the planning process works, the best time to use, and the types of stations to select. Are you ready?

Sequenced Flip

If you want to present content to your students and have them practice it in a particular order, consider using the sequenced in-class flip (Figure 5.1).

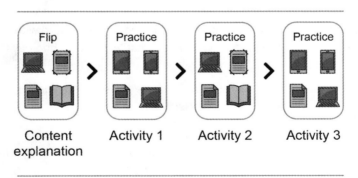

Figure 5.1 Sequenced in-class flip.

The sequenced in-class flip consists of many stations that follow a linear order. All students start at the same flip station, completing the interdependent tasks that follow (Ramirez, 2017). In a sequenced flip of four stations, students will start at the first station and finish at the fourth station. Students must finish one task before moving to the next.

This type of configuration is ideal for teaching new content. You can use the sequenced in-class flip with a large number of students, as long as the classroom space allows duplicate stations.

We recommend that the sequenced in-class flip consist mainly of flip and practice stations. However, if the teacher decides that students can move at their own pace, an independent station could be added at the end of the sequence. Or, a feedback station could be the last station in the sequence.

For her public speaking course, Martha used this configuration to teach a group of eighteen high school students how to create diagrams. She planned three stations:

1. The first one had the explanation of a diagram.
2. The second had a written description that students had to visualize into a diagram.
3. The third contained laptops for students to use to collaborate and create a digital diagram.

With eighteen students in the classroom, six long tables were necessary. At the first two tables, nine students worked alone with the material. At the next two tables, students worked in groups of three. At the last two tables, the same groups worked on laptops.

For a more detailed account of Martha's lesson, read about it in her blog by scanning the QR code or visiting the URL: **bit.ly/2CeDYa9**.

If you have a large class and wonder how this in-class flip might fit your lessons, then duplicating stations (shown in Figure 5.2) is your best option.

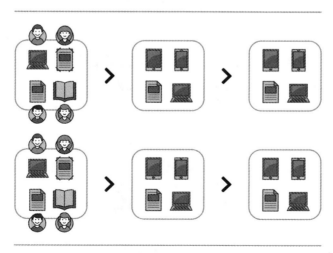

Figure 5.2. Duplicated sequenced stations.

For example, you can divide a group of thirty-two students into four smaller groups and place them in identical flip stations (Station 1). In this way, the teacher can monitor the smaller groups as they work on each task. The duplication of stations will vary according to how the teacher has planned the work in each one. Accordingly, more stations can be set up if you think eight students is too much (we do). Another option is the division of workspaces within one station, as shown in Figure 5.3.

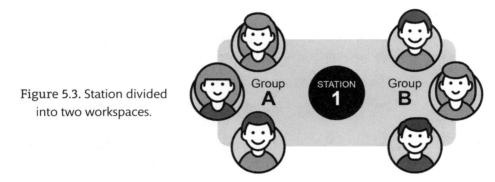

Figure 5.3. Station divided into two workspaces.

In Figure 5.3, we can see how one station is divided into two groups of three students each, instead of using it for one group of six. This is a good way of optimizing station areas with large classes.

Even though in-class flips include flip and practice stations, this configuration can vary: stations with only flipped content, or stations with flipped content and practice activities. See Figure 5.4 for a sequenced in-class flip example we planned for a group of thirty teachers in a teacher-training workshop that contained a duplicated sequence of two flip stations.

Figure 5.4. Duplicated, sequenced in-class flip with flip stations.

In this teacher-training workshop about flipped learning and the in-class flip, we planned two flip stations. Station 1 contained a flipped learning video with a worksheet. Station 2 had a mini-poster display with an explanation of the in-class flip along with a graphic organizer to complete (Figure 5.5). Knowing there could be up to thirty attendees, we decided to duplicate the stations, for a total of four stations. That way, the thirty attendees were divided into four groups and distributed among the stations (with between seven and eight attendees in each station). For better organization, we decided to time the stations, using an alarm to indicate when people were expected to switch. When the alarm went off, the two groups in Station 1 switched to Station 2 and vice-versa. Watch a video of the lesson by scanning the QR code or visiting the URL: **bit.ly/2ODF5SY**.

Figure 5.5. In-class flip workshop.

Tips for sequenced stations

- *The first station should provide flipped content.*
- *Time station rotations to achieve the maximum level of focus possible.*
- *Use an alarm to alert students when to rotate.*
- *The order of stations matters, so confirm that the complexity of tasks in the various stations is gradual or at the same level.*
- *Plan an independent station if students move at their own pace.*

- *You may use this configuration to focus entirely on flipped content, provided you plan accountability activities within the stations.*

- *Ask students to write a playlist of songs they like. As students work on the last flip station rotation, play the playlist that helps with the overall ambiance of the lesson.*

TEACHING SPOTLIGHT

Paola Cardona is an English teacher in Manizales, Colombia, who uses Edmodo in her in-class flip language lessons. Read how she navigates six stations:

1. **Video:** Students watch a video and reflect on a question that they later share with their group members.

2. **Vocabulary:** Students work on exercises such as association, matching, Pictionary, etc.

3. **Listening:** Students complete different listening exercises such as fill in the gaps, match, give opinions, etc.

4. **Reading and Writing:** Students answer a thought-provoking question in a subgroup in Edmodo and receive feedback from other group members.

5. **Oral Production:** Discussions, debates, open questions, mini interviews, etc., happen here. According to Paola, "This station is a little intimidating sometimes, depending on students' language level, but it is one of the most rewarding ones. Here, I can really see my students speaking, trying their best to communicate. Edmodo here is crucial, because they sometimes post their voice notes with questions to the subgroups, and their peers answer them."

6. **"English is fun" independent station:** Extra activities are provided for early finishers. Students can dive deeper into the challenges Edmodo frequently offers.

We agree with Paola when she says, "Don't be afraid to flip your lessons; it can flip your life as an educator, too!"

Looped Flip

In the looped in-class flip, students can start at any station, provided they complete every one of them and close the loop. Activities in each station should offer the same level of complexity so that learners can start anywhere. This is different from the previous configuration, since the sequenced in-class flip is linear, which means all students start at the same station and move forward. In the looped configuration, the flip station can be inside or outside the loop. The decision to include the flip station will depend on the specific aims of the lesson and whether learners know the content.

The looped in-class flip is as good for reviewing old content as it is for presenting new content.

If you have already introduced a topic, but you worry that some students might still need to remember content while working on practice stations, this is an ideal configuration. In this case, the flipped station can stay outside the loop; that way, students can rotate through the practice stations and go to the flipped station if needed. If, on the contrary, you want to introduce new topics, it's a good idea to place the flip station inside the loop. We will explain these two options in more detail below.

Flip Station Inside the Loop

Including the flip station inside the loop is a good idea when introducing new content. You can do this in different ways. The key to having flip stations within the loop is that the content is independent of or complementary to what you expect students to do in the practice stations. Avoid any interdependent tasks with this type of configuration.

Let's see how this works with an example. In Figure 5.6, we see a loop created with two flip stations and three practice stations. So let's say a science teacher is demonstrating the water cycle to her class. She has planned three stations with different tasks:

Station 1: Water cycle diagram creation

Station 2: Water cycle description worksheet

Station 3: Water cycle online game

Other tasks could include quizzes, apps, a terrarium, etc. Here students show mastery of what they know about the water cycle.

In our example, students can begin at any station. We have two flip stations, which are independent of or complementary to the main topic, the water cycle, so that rotation can be fluid. Students do not need the content in the flip station to complete the practice station activities. However, it might be helpful for them to understand the topic more thoroughly. An example of a flip station with independent content for this lesson could be an explanation of an upcoming new topic. Moreover, an example of a flip station with complementary content could be a reading activity with fun facts about the water cycle.

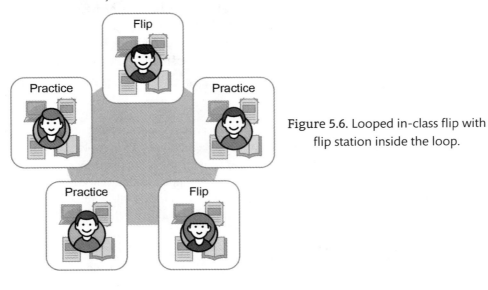

Figure 5.6. Looped in-class flip with flip station inside the loop.

Another example of a loop setup for new content could contain only flip stations with accountability activities (see Figure 5.7).

In her language pedagogy class, Carolina wanted her students to learn how to teach content in English through different pedagogical approaches. She designed four stations.

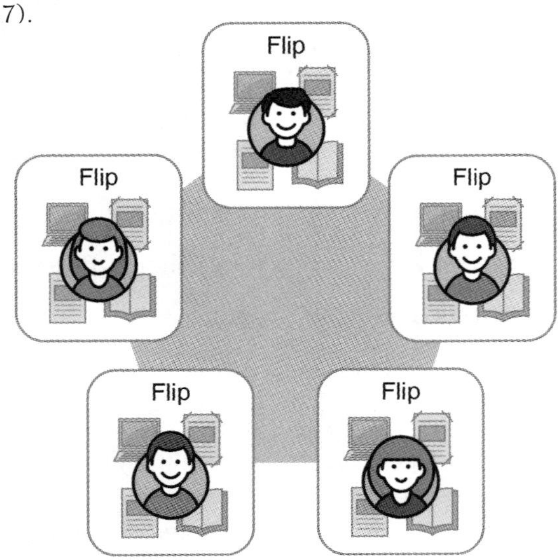

Figure 5.7. Looped in-class flip with flip stations only.

TABLE 5.1

Stations with different teaching approaches

STATION	CONTENT	ACTIVITY DESCRIPTION
Station 1	Use SIOP (the Sheltered Instruction Observation Protocol).	Watch a video sample of how the SIOP model does the lesson delivery.
Station 2	Teach through CLIL (Content and Language Integrated Learning).	Jigsaw reading about the definition and the different components.
Station 3	How to teach with CBI (Content-Based Instruction).	Watch a video lecture about the model and take notes.
Station 4	Lesson plan samples.	Analyze different lesson plan formats and identify similarities and differences between the three.

We have now seen how a loop configuration works with the flip station within the loop. Now let's see how it works with the flip station outside the loop.

Flip Station Outside the Loop

Planning the lesson with the flip station outside the loop becomes ideal when students already have some familiarity with the content. This configuration is great for reviews or right after teaching new content. You can distribute students among the stations for them to work on each activity until they are back to square one. The use of a timer is a good idea to control rotation timing.

You will decide whether to include the flip station inside or outside the loop based on students' previous knowledge of the content. Activities in practice stations will build upon the content in the flip station. If students have already learned the content in a previous class or have done it as homework, then the role of the flip station outside the loop is to refresh and review the information.

If students missed the explanation in the previous class or didn't do the homework, the flip station outside the loop will help them cope with the activities inside the loop, which helps you differentiate instruction.

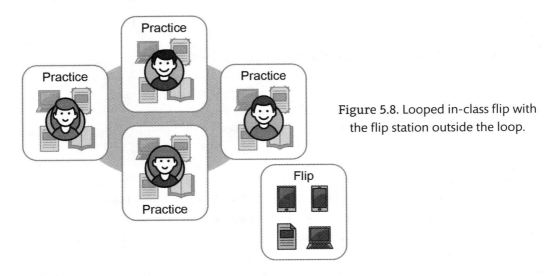

Figure 5.8. Looped in-class flip with the flip station outside the loop.

Independent Stations in Looped In-Class Flips

Just as in the sequenced in-class flip, including an independent station in the looped configuration is an effective response for high achievers. The independent station will always sit outside the loop, since it will provide extra activities for students to work on after they have finished the activities within the cycle. Some ideas for an independent station could include a game, a summarizing activity (writing or doodling), a hands-on creating task, etc.

As you can see, there are many possibilities for this type of in-class flip according to different needs and learning objectives.

Figure 5.9 shows an example of a station plan with two flip stations outside the loop and four practice stations. There are two different types of flipped content for this configuration.

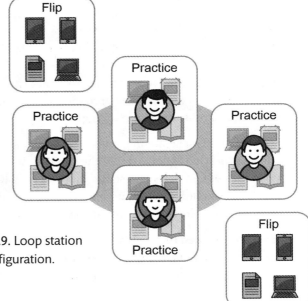

Figure 5.9. Loop station configuration.

Tips for looped stations:

- *Looped configurations are excellent for content reviews.*
- *Timing station rotation works well with flip stations inside the loop.*
- *When the flip station is outside the loop, students should feel free to access the flip station anytime.*
- *Plan activities at a complexity level that allows students to work at any station, regardless of the station at which they started.*
- *Offering independent stations is a good idea for high achievers when students are not timed.*
- *Plan independent stations outside the loop.*
- *It is always a good idea to include a feedback station, which should go outside the loop.*

Mixed Flip

The mixed flip configuration works well for mixed-level classes where students' background knowledge varies. It offers flexibility and choice, so you can use it to offer differentiation to your class. If some of your students master the content, but others still need more support, use this configuration. Also, this configuration is a great choice when you need to address more than one concept.

This configuration offers students the possibility to move at their own pace and also to decide where they need to go. Those who are behind can catch up, and those who are ahead can keep on moving forward.

The mixed in-class flip requires flip, practice, and independent stations. So "students who need instruction will start at the flip station [and] those who previously know the content will skip the flip stations and start at the practice stations" (Ramirez, 2016, fig. 3). Also,

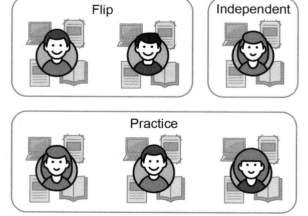

Figure 5.10. Mixed in-class flip.

49

free student movement among the stations helps learning to flow. Offering independent stations can offer extra learning opportunities for students. They can work at the independent station while the practice stations are full.

The number of stations will vary according to the number of students, the space, and your teaching objectives. Keep in mind that "some students might know the content of one flip station and not another, and some might need to step back and review content explanations, so their flow sequence varies according to previous knowledge and needs" (Ramirez, 2017, fig. 3).

Martha planned a mixed setup for a group of twenty-four university students in an English-speaking course. The topics they were learning included how to pronounce regular verbs in past tense (with /t/, /d/, and /ed/ sounds—e.g., *worked, lived, wanted*) and –s endings (with /s/, /z/, and /iz/ sounds). Martha's students were at different speaking levels. Some were at a high level due to prior experience with the language (students who had come from bilingual schools, a few who had lived abroad). Many more were at a lower level of proficiency (those who had learned most of their English while at the university). So, you can imagine how the lesson was relevant for some and not so much for others.

Additionally, Martha discovered that some students did not use the past tense very well, but this grammar topic was old, so it was not in her syllabus. How could she plan a lesson that would fulfill these different needs? She planned a mixed in-class flip with seven stations (see Figure 5.11) that would tackle the two pronunciation topics plus the grammar topic. In this example, the stations were numbered 1 to 7; however, we suggest using names instead of numbers to clarify the station topic at a glance.

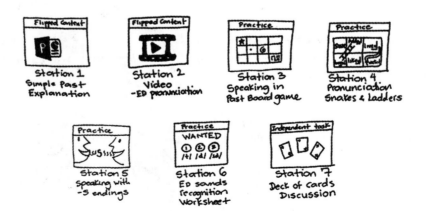

Figure 5.11. Mixed in-class flip for pronunciation.

Let's take a closer look. Stations 1 and 2 were the flip stations, with content for the past tense and the rules for pronunciation. Station 1 featured a PowerPoint slideshow with explanations. Station 2 offered a YouTube video with the rules of pronunciation of regular verbs in the past. Stations 3, 4, and 6 were practice stations, offering worksheets with answer keys for students to check on their own. Station 5 was also a practice station. It had a speaking practice activity, and it offered a mini poster with pronunciation rules as a reference. Station 7 was the independent station, offering a discussion card game that had no prerequisite within the station rotation. In this way, Martha ensured review of the three topics, and students could choose where to go depending on their needs.

While planning this lesson, Martha wondered what would happen if students were not sure where they should go. The solution? A checklist, shown in Figure 5.12. To provide organization and choice, she gave them a checklist to mark what stations they needed to go to. In this particular configuration, Martha planned more stations than students could cover during the eighty-minute class, but she encouraged them to work on at least four stations within the class period. This removed pressure from students to finish it all and allowed them to work and learn at their own pace.

Station work checklist		
Name:		
1	PPT	Simple past tense powerpoint explanation (optional)	
2	YouTube	Pronunciation of regular verbs in past video (optional)	
3		Speaking in past: boardgame	
4		Pronouncing in past: Snakes n ladders	
5		Speaking with –s endings	✓
6	/d/ /t/ /ɪd/	ED sounds recognition worksheet	
7		Deck of cards discussion (optional)	

Icons from: flaticon.com

Figure 5.12. Checklist for student self-pacing in an in-class flip about pronunciation.

For more detail on Martha's lesson, read her reflections in her blog post by scanning the QR code or visiting the URL: **bit.ly/3eB4wPX**

When planning a mixed in-class flip, you might consider the following aspects:

- When you give students a minimum number of stations to work on, plan activities in such a way that students don't miss out on the other stations.

- The more stations students work on, the more they practice and consolidate what they have learned.

- Get to know your students so that you can plan station activities they need and want.

- Number and/or label stations to clarify their organization for students as they move from one to the other.

Tips for mixed stations:

- *Give students a checklist to keep track of the stations they should visit.*
- *Provide answer keys for students to check their understanding independently.*
- *Plan more stations than students can cover in a class period.*
- *Independent stations are ideal in this configuration.*
- *Number or name stations to facilitate student rotation.*
- *Include a feedback station.*

TEACHING SPOTLIGHT

Jeff Magoto is a computer-assisted language learning (CALL) teacher educator at the University of Oregon in Eugene, Oregon, U.S.A. Since Jeff teaches graduate students who are teachers themselves, he has an important mission: to model best practices in his own classroom. Like many, he was looking for an alternative pedagogy that didn't rely on out-of-class work. He was especially curious to see how in-class flips promoted and inspired student agency and autonomy.

Jeff has worked with different forms of the in-class flip. For a teacher training session on "Talking about the weather in Brazil," he designed an in-class flip for teachers of many languages (who neither spoke nor studied Portuguese, but had a background in

Spanish). He used a mixed configuration, which was great for offering choice, but not so good for "crowd control." Students gravitated to stations 1 to 3, which were low-order thinking skills (LOTS) tasks and required technology. Jeff says, "They didn't have enough facilitation or technology for them in all of the stations, so they chose to work only in the easiest ones." So, if he could have changed the configuration, he would have used a duplicate sequenced one, which would have solved the problem of too many students at certain stations.

Jeff believes these are the main benefits of the in-class flip:

1. It takes the "time–space" shift of flipped learning in new directions.

2. It supports both parallel and linear learning experiences.

3. Stations can be structured and less structured, simple and challenging, with our without technology.

4. Teachers and learners rediscover the motivating power of personalized paths to learning.

5. It encourages experimentation, such as creating stations in the halls, courtyards, and adjacent classrooms.

6. Assessment, especially formative assessment, is a more natural part of the learning progression.

Half 'n' Half Flip

Use the half 'n' half configuration if your class meets one of these three conditions:

1. Tutoring is necessary.

2. Student learning levels are different.

3. Teacher support is necessary.

In this configuration, you divide the group into two big stations: a flip station and a teacher support station. The role of the teacher here is to tutor and give feedback and more personalized support to half of the class, while the other half is studying the flipped content. When the time is up, the groups switch. This way, the teacher has tutored or supported the whole class by the end of the lesson. Still, switching the groups in one class session will depend on the specific needs presented by the students.

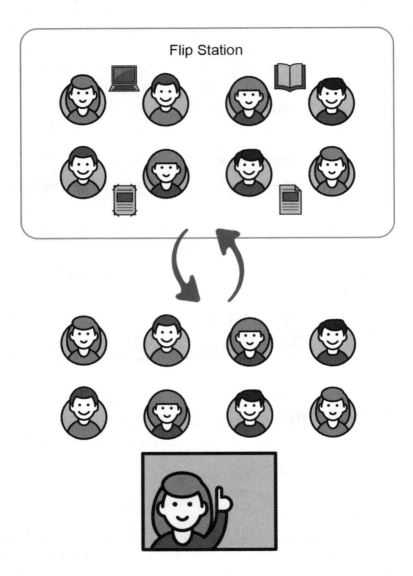

Figure 5.13. Half 'n' half configuration.

You can plan this type of flip for new content or for reviews. We have used this type of configuration with our small language-learning and content classes.

The half 'n' half configuration has interesting uses within the group learning space, such as peer instruction, in-class tutoring, and feedback. Can you think of any others? Are you intrigued by how you can use this configuration? Let us walk you through it.

TEACHING SPOTLIGHT

Randy Brown is a teacher in Monroe School District in Monroe, Washington, U.S.A, who used the in-class flip to reduce the teacher-to-student ratio by fifty percent in his math class. He has recorded more than one hundred math videos over the years. In Randy's in-class flip, half of the class is watching a math video while the other half is working one-on-one with him in guided practice activities. Then they switch. See it for yourself by scanning the QR code or visiting the URL: **bit.ly/30eTASE**

For Randy, the half 'n' half configuration has many benefits:

- It helps eliminate behavior problems.
- It offers valuable one-on-one tutoring sessions.
- Students can re-watch the content video as many times as necessary.
- Parents can watch the video from home and help their child.
- Absent students don't miss anything.

Randy shares his best practices with the half 'n' half flip:

- Create your own high-quality videos.
- Use great classroom management skills so that the fifty percent of students working independently stay focused.
- Spend quality time with struggling students.
- Share videos with parents and email them daily if students' assignments are missing.

Using Peer Instruction with the Half 'n' Half Flip

So how does the half 'n' half in-class flip configuration facilitate peer instruction? Peer instruction presents interesting challenges to students. Students understand concepts more thoroughly when challenged to explain them to someone. The additional responsibility of making their peers understand pushes students to dive more deeply into their knowledge. In our case, we have asked students to teach each other language, so our approach to peer instruction varies from Mazur's proposal, explained below. Since in language learning there are often no right or wrong answers, we create our own rules for peer instruction when we apply it in an in-class flip.

In Mazur's model, he asks a question (multiple choice or yes/no) and projects it on a screen. Then students commit to an answer and mark it using clickers. The teacher hopes for half of the students to get it right and the other half to get it wrong for peer instruction to succeed. Students discuss their answers and try to convince each other they have the right answer. Afterwards the teacher asks a similar question, hoping to see an increase in response accuracy, and then the process repeats.

In our case, we don't ask a question but rather assign a topic and provide the resources (in class) for students to learn and understand. In this stage of the lesson, the teacher is available to clarify and support students as they learn the material. Then, students work together and teach each other their topic. Half of the students teach each other the content while the other half of the students work with the teacher in understanding the information provided. Then, they switch.

To wrap up, the teacher asks some questions to ensure everybody understood the topic. Finally, students all move back to the half 'n' half configuration. This time, one group of students works on a set task, and the other group works with a different task, but the teacher is available to help both groups. This variation of the half 'n' half flip and of peer instruction has resulted in an interesting approach for us. Do you see possibilities for your own context?

Using peer instruction as a strategy can help teachers craft better learning experiences for their students, whether it is in a half 'n' half configuration or in other ways.

Dividing the Group for Tutoring

Homogeneous classes, in which all students are at the same learning level, are atypical. Classes are mostly multilevel, and it is hard to accommodate all learners. The half 'n' half flip provides a way to divide the class into two groups so that the teacher may tutor the ones that need it. In the meantime, the other group works on their own, and then they switch. With this strategy, the teacher can always support closely those who need it.

Let's say you have a class where part of your students are up to speed with a topic you have been teaching, yet others are still not getting it. You can do different exercises with a half 'n' half configuration, depending on your intention with the content. The configuration will change depending on whether you are reviewing or introducing content.

In a review class, you can offer content at the flip station to the up-to-speed group, while you work more personally with the students who need more support. You can choose to switch groups, depending on how much tutoring students need and the duration of your class. You could dedicate the whole class period to the lower level students, while the higher-level students continue to review on their own. You can solve issues with the lower-level students, provide one-on-one feedback, and assign practice activities.

For students who are up to speed, you can provide new content as well. While they are in the application phase of learning, you can monitor and provide support. Please note that if you plan to devote an entire lesson to tutoring half of the class, the flip station needs to have accountability activities for successful autonomous work. You would also need to design your lesson to fit the whole class time.

Going back to the review lesson scenario, when students switch groups, the tutored students would review the content at the flip station while the teacher works with the higher-level students. The lower-level students will need a higher level of support compared to the higher-level group. This does not necessarily mean that the flip station will have a completely different complexity level, though this is a great option to differentiate according to learning levels.

Imagine the same group of students with a lesson designed to introduce new content, instead of reviewing it. Let's say you were teaching the verb *to be*. Half of your group is struggling with understanding the negative forms of *be* (isn't, aren't, am not), but the other half has shown mastery and could move on to interrogative sentences, which is the next step in this topic. Because the setup is a half 'n' half flip, you could differentiate the content in various ways. One way is by allowing half of the class to advance and the other half to continue reviewing. Another option is planning for half of the class to advance in the new topic with the teacher and the other half to do it more independently with the flipped content. The way the teacher can tutor and provide support will vary.

Tips for Half 'n' Half Stations

- *Plan clear, autonomous, well-scaffolded tasks for the autonomous half of learners. When students are working on their own, they need clarity. The teacher will not be available to them during the time she is with the other half of the group.*

- *There should be a clear outcome for the individual/group work at the station where the teacher is not present.*

- *Plan how you will group students to work with you.*

- *Plan clear tasks for students' time with you.*

- *It's a good idea to involve parents by sending the videos home so they can watch them and assist their kids with the work as well (when applicable to the context).*

Planning station-work in-class flips involves working through logistics and having an eye for detail. A good in-class flip lesson has stations that:

- Respond to students' needs.

- Have a clear teaching goal.

- Have a clear learning purpose that leads to the teaching goal.

Avoid planning station work for every class, since there is a significant amount of time that comes with preparing each lesson. Moreover, variety in teaching creates the "wow" factor of a dynamic and active student-centered class. If you still don't want to be at the center of the room, you can plan in-situ (non-station) in-class flips more frequently. You don't have to turn your classroom upside down every time.

REFLECTIVE PAUSE

What type of station configuration you could start using tomorrow in your own teaching situation?

THE IN-CLASS FLIP AROUND THE WORLD

"My whole year nine science class is an in-class flip. I have video lessons on a learning management system, and I have a workbook that contains pre-video and post-video questions, exercises, and experiments. The workbook also contains templates for writing Cornell notes for each video. The students work at their own pace. When they get to class, they open their workbook and the LMS and find where they are. They then get started. I walk around the classroom interacting with every student, every lesson, every day. I check where the students are in the lesson, I check the quality of their notes, I check their answers, I look for misconceptions, I answer questions, I re-teach concepts, and I encourage my students. The students do the experiments as stations when they are ready. Each week, I assign mastery quizzes that are self-marked."

Here is a QR code and link to a video I made about my workbook: **bit.ly/30k2ApH**

—Steve Griffiths, chemistry teacher, Brisbane, Queensland, Australia

CHAPTER **6**

Differentiating Instruction with the In-Class Flip

> **This chapter addresses several ISTE Standards:**
>
> **2.1. Learner**
> Educators continually improve their practice by learning from and with others and exploring proven and promising practices that leverage technology to improve student learning. Educators:
>
> *a. Set professional learning goals to explore and apply pedagogical approaches made possible by technology and reflect on their effectiveness.*
>
> *c. Stay current with research that supports improved student learning outcomes, including findings from the learning sciences.*
>
> **2.2. Leader**
> Educators seek out opportunities for leadership to support student empowerment and success and to improve teaching and learning. Educators:
>
> *b. Advocate for equitable access to educational technology, digital content, and learning opportunities to meet the diverse needs of all students.*

2.4. Collaborator

Educators dedicate time to collaborate with both colleagues and students to improve practice, discover and share resources and ideas, and solve problems. Educators:

b. Collaborate and co-learn with students to discover and use new digital resources and diagnose and troubleshoot technology issues.

c. Use collaborative tools to expand students' authentic, real-world learning experiences by engaging virtually with experts, teams, and students, locally and globally.

2.5. Designer

Educators design authentic, learner-driven activities and environments that recognize and accommodate learner variability. Educators:

a. Use technology to create, adapt, and personalize learning experiences that foster independent learning and accommodate learner differences and needs.

2.7. Analyst

Educators understand and use data to drive their instruction and support students in achieving their learning goals. Educators:

a. Provide alternative ways for students to demonstrate competency and reflect on their learning using technology.

b. Use technology to design and implement a variety of formative and summative assessments that accommodate learner needs, provide timely feedback to students, and inform instruction.

IN-CLASS FLIPPING HAS LED US TO BETTER TEACHING, because it has inevitably challenged us to plan, problem solve, be creative, keep our students in mind, and create connections with each one of them. The in-class flip is one of the vehicles you can use to provide meaningful, active, and differentiated learning. Once you take your first test drive, you won't regret it.

Good teachers are always looking for strategies and techniques to make learning easier for students. That's how we found flipped learning and the in-class flip in the first place. Even so, the task of offering a meaningful learning experience for all can seem like an epic battle. Some reasons behind this conflict are the amount of content to teach, standardized testing, and large classrooms. Other reasons include the variety in our students' contexts, interests, and readiness levels.

Differentiating Instruction

Teachers use many strategies to solve students' difficulties and create optimal learning situations. Differentiated instruction and flipped learning are just two of those effective strategies. The in-class flip is an easy way to seamlessly integrate flipped learning and differentiated instruction. This integration benefits all students, since it provides the time within the group learning space to take learning to a new level. In an in-class flip, students are at the center, and the teacher acts as a true facilitator and designer of meaningful and long-lasting learning experiences.

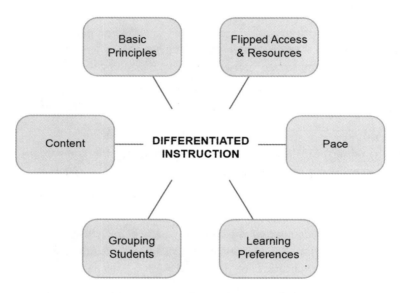

Figure 6.1. Differentiated instruction.

The Basics and Principles

Differentiated instruction is not new. It was born out of the need to address students' differences and offer them each a meaningful learning experience. According to Carol Tomlinson, a pioneer of differentiated instruction, "Differentiation means tailoring instruction to meet individual needs" (Tomlinson, n.d., para. 1).

This agrees with Flipped Learning Network (2014, I.3), which states that the teacher "differentiates to make content accessible and relevant to all students." You can design a differentiated classroom as part of an in-class flip. We will show you how in the following sections.

In Carol Tomlinson's model for differentiation, four curricular elements can be differentiated: content, product, process, and learning environment. Let us break this down based on Tomlinson's words:

- Content refers to "the information and ideas students grapple with to reach the learning goals."

- Process relates to "how students take in and make sense of the content."

- Product is "how students show what they know, understand, and can do."

- Learning environment refers to "the climate or tone of the classroom." (Tomlinson, n.d., p. 20).

These elements are not always easy to integrate within a traditional teaching paradigm.

How can a teacher offer many ways for learners to access content or to show their knowledge if he or she is in front of the classroom lecturing? In his Flipped Learning 3.0 Differentiation Strategies course, Jon Bergmann mentions that "we need to change the fundamental structure of how we teach." By flipping our class, we can truly cater to our students' different needs and interests. It is only by shifting the way we teach that we can truly differentiate.

Differentiation and Flipping

Undoubtedly, flipped learning and differentiation make a good team. Flipping prepares the way for differentiation. It allows the teacher to free up class time to apply different strategies for learning. It also offers the possibility to have a closer view of learners as individuals. When you flip, you get a better grasp of students' learning processes; their level of understanding; and their interests, preferences, and personalities. The in-class flip creates learning spaces and teaching opportunities that allow differentiation in every lesson.

We are not the only ones who have seen this connection. In their book *The Differentiated Flipped Classroom*, Carbaugh and Doubet describe this relationship as a "logical synergy between these two models [since] the flipped environment provides rich opportunities to cater to diversity because of the flexibility linked to its use" (p. xxi). Flipping allows the creation of "a rich environment in which to actively cultivate differentiation" (p. 8). Differentiation is crucial in today's classroom, and the in-class flip makes it feasible.

Teachers can include more than content, product, and process in an in-class flip lesson. The list of options to differentiate includes access, resources, pace, learning preference, grouping, content, choice, feedback, student support, and mastery. Get ready to learn how to differentiate with the in-class flip through the stories of teachers who have done it successfully.

Access and Resources

Classrooms, like students around the world, can differ considerably. Some schools have an overabundance of resources, amazing infrastructures, and enormous libraries. Other schools may have none of these. Even so, both can put meaningful learning experiences at the top of their priority list. With an in-class flip, teachers can differentiate instruction regardless of their economic conditions and lack of resources.

When planning a class, the teacher has to decide on the content to deliver and the tasks to perform. In a traditional classroom, every student has to access content in the same way and at the same time, and has to perform more or less the same tasks. This creates barriers in learning for low-achievers or students with learning difficulties, and it bores high achievers to death. During an in-class flip, teachers can add a variety of resources and types of access within the classroom walls so that students may use their preferred tools and ways to approach content.

Teachers can use different electronic (smartphones, tablets, laptops, etc.) and non-electronic (books, worksheets, papers, beakers, models, blueprints, etc.) tools to guarantee every student's access to the material in their preferred way. If the teacher is not at the center of the classroom as the only source of content, then students can have more freedom to access content in their own way.

Take Mr. Lopes' in-class flip plan, for example. While teaching the topic of the planets to students, Lopes needs to integrate science concepts and language arts. His classroom is small, and he has only limited resources available: an encyclopedia, his smartphone and tablet, and a presentation station in the classroom (an overhead projector). He has planned for students to do some research about the topic, and he has found some incredible resources he would like to suggest to students. Also, he expects them to show their knowledge of the names of the planets, their particular traits, and the order in which they are located in the solar system. He has only a forty-five-minute lesson to complete the assignment. What does he do? He sets up an in-class flip!

In his planning, Mr. Lopes offers students a cool video he found online (Storybots singing a rap song about the planets). He also found a cute book titled *Life in Space* that has brief explanations of each one of the planets. He Googled the topic and found a plethora of free worksheets; he plans to use three of those because they help with his goals. His own presentation of the planets is pretty cool—students have loved his slideshow about the planets every year, so he wants to use that too. And, of course, he has to use the assigned textbook since it was bought by parents, and they would give him a hard time if they saw him using external materials.

With his in-class flip, Mr. Lopes' lesson can be organized by stations, where every station contains one of the materials featuring the same content in a distinct mode, allowing each student to choose the option that best fits her style. The teacher can provide some adjustments to guarantee that students' resources aid differentiation. For example, he can adapt the worksheets, tiering them at different levels of complexity for every student to work on the material that fits their readiness level. He can also decide whether every student has to go to every station, or if there are multiple routes to achieve the lesson objectives. In an in-class flip, as you plan activities and resources with your students' needs in mind, you create a differentiated learning experience.

REFLECTIVE PAUSE

Draw what you think Mr. Lopes's in-class flip configuration could look like. Consider the mentioned materials and the fact that he has three ELL students who struggle with the English language.

Pace

Understanding concepts and internalizing them are processes that vary from student to student. Unfortunately, our one-size-fits-all educational systems ignore differences in learning pace. Allowing students to move at their own pace within a strict curriculum with high standards becomes a difficult task. With the in-class flip, you can differentiate the pace at which students explore content. You can account for learning in every single lesson, yet allow students to own their learning and enjoy the educational materials.

Take Mrs. Colbert's case as an example. Mrs. Colbert teaches third-grade math. She is working on the concepts of word problems and place/value. Even though sixty percent of her students understand mathematical concepts with no difficulty, approximately forty percent still struggle with addition and subtraction. She wants to differentiate her class, but she doesn't know how to do it for everybody. She created some instructional videos on the new topics (word problems and place/value), but she is afraid if she sends them home for students to watch on their own, they will get confused. So she decided to do an in-class flip.

She split the class into two, gave the videos to one half of the class, and then sat with the rest to check understanding of addition and subtraction. Then, she paired students from both groups and had students from the watching team explain the new concepts to the other students. That way, the students who watch the videos in class are accountable for the learning they do while watching, and the ones whom the teacher tutors get exposure to the new concepts. Mrs. Colbert then plans an activity for all the students, having them apply the new concepts to ensure they all understand them. The result? Her students were understanding the different topics fully and at their own pace.

REFLECTIVE PAUSE

Think of your most complex unit in terms of pacing. What topic causes students to struggle at different levels? How could an in-class flip help you?

Learning Preferences

For years, teachers have tried to include their students' preferences in the learning process. However, a few years ago, an interesting debate emerged in the field of neuroscience regarding the term "learning style." Its implications for education also emerged. It left educators the world over petrified.

Scan the code or visit the URL to read the article "Teachers must ditch 'neuromyth' of learning styles, say scientists" from *The Guardian* (subject to availability): **bit. ly/30nfpQg**

This debate suggests that by trying to cater to the different learning styles (visual, auditory, and kinesthetic), teachers may be harming students instead of serving them well. An article that appeared in The Guardian in 2017 suggested that teachers might be depriving students of being exposed to more effective learning strategies. Even though we are aware of the debate, and we agree, we can't deny students have strong preferences for materials they like to use. It is therefore important to offer them a multiplicity of learning artifacts.

When planning a class, it is important and beneficial to have different kinds of educational materials. Texts, audios, videos, board games, tasks, lab equipment, globes, maps, balls, nets, rackets, and more can ensure we meet students' interests and needs. We don't want to label students and give them only one way of accessing information. We want to plan different types of activities so that all students feel engaged throughout the lesson. By paying special attention to students' differing needs from the outset, we can offer a learning experience that interests every student and helps them feel more in control of their learning process.

Sometimes, students center their attention on complying with tasks they are assigned. They do this not because they feel they will learn from those tasks, but because the teacher created them, and they feel they must do what the teacher says. In an in-class flip environment, student choice is crucial to achieve high levels of engagement and deeper learning. By including resources that interest students, teachers create empowered and motivated learners.

Let's examine Ms. Dentici's case. Ms. Dentici teaches in a rural school in the south of Italy. She has twenty-six learners in her seventh-grade art classroom. She has planned to teach them about different representations of art through Greek mythology. Because of the different learning preferences of her students, she planned an in-class flip using stations.

Ms. Dentici started by asking students to watch a movie about Greek mythology over the weekend. The movies on the list of options were *The Legend of Hercules*, *Percy Jackson & the Olympians: The Lightning Thief*, *Clash of the Titans*, *Wrath of the Titans*, and *Troy*. Ms. Dentici expected students to watch any R-rated movie with their parents. She asked students to watch the movie of their choice and to take notes on the main features of scenery, the use of ships and carriages, and the role of women, and to choose their favorite mythological creature. Students were excited for the weekend's task. Ms. Dentici was dubious about whether students would come prepared on the following Monday. So, just in case they hadn't, she prepared a station where students could watch clips of *Hercules* (the Disney version). On Monday, she found that most students had watched the movies because this pre-work was exciting. Ms. Dentici prepared five stations; three with "traditional arts" and three with "alternative arts." At the traditional arts stations, students could choose to paint, sculpt, or draw their favorite mythological creature. At the alternative stations, students could draw a cartoon, write a haiku, or record a video using props she had brought. Students were ecstatic about the activity and participated actively.

With her in-class flip, Ms. Dentici had time to talk to students about the different art techniques while at their stations. She prepared a handout for each station where she had:

- the main materials used in each different artistic representation.

- a short biography of the most salient artist in producing each form of art.

- a brief explanation of the history of painting, sculpture, drawing, cartoons, poetry, and audio-visual production.

Ms. Dentici locked the art project materials in a trunk. To unlock it, students had to share information from their handout with the others at their station. Students had lots of fun. They learned about different forms of art. Also, each one of them got a chance to represent their favorite Greek mythological creature through varied art forms.

REFLECTIVE PAUSE

How can the use of students' learning preferences in terms of style and materials help you craft more engaging or interesting lessons?

Grouping students

Regardless of the teaching context, the way you group students can determine how well the lesson transpires. We have had students who prefer to work with their closest friends because they don't get along with certain other classmates. We have had situations where not all students in a group are doing the work. And, unfortunately, we've had classes where bullying occurred.

Grouping can affect the outcome of the lesson depending on age groups and cultural backgrounds, among other reasons. As a result, careful planning around how to group students is also part of our teaching. In-class flipping has allowed us to explore many ways to learn. What is more, we have gained a wider view of how students interact, their level of understanding, their interests, and the pace at which they work. These gains are a result of monitoring and having constant teacher-student interaction.

We have found different recommended practices for flexible grouping from different authors. They tend to arrive at the same conclusion: grouping students in different ways is beneficial to them and their learning process. For example, in their book, *The Differentiated Flipped Classroom*, Carbaugh and Doubet define flexible grouping as "the use of multiple grouping strategies in a relatively short amount of time" (p. 14). More simply, Cox (n.d.) describes it as "a range of grouping students together for delivering instruction" (para. 5).

We also need to consider the different organizations of students within the class period. For example, for Carolyn Coil (2009), grouping can be homogeneous, heterogeneous, whole class, individualized, or paired. So, when you include student grouping in your day-to-day plan, differentiation is also taking place. Using variables such as student preference, level of readiness, interests, friendship, gender, and personality can help you populate the groups. The biggest benefit of flexibility in grouping is "[getting] learners used to work with virtually every member of their class" (p. 17). It develops social skills and contributes to positive student relationships and cooperative learning.

Let's see how flexible grouping can work in different ways. Within a classroom where you have created a safe and stress-free environment, randomized grouping will work. Students who feel comfortable with the teacher, the group, and their capacities won't mind with whom they have to work and will focus on getting the work done.

Randomizing techniques that teachers can include in different classes are:

- Counting consecutively and then asking students to group with peers who have their same number. You can do this with colors, animals, vocabulary, expressions, etc.

- Using colored pieces of paper, popsicle sticks, matching cards, or different candy types.

The in-class flip allows for variations in grouping to take place within one lesson. With this in mind, consider how and when you need students to work in groups within the planning process. Coil (2009) recommends changing the way you group learners within one class. Therefore, a lesson should include, when possible, a variation of individual, pair, and group work.

REFLECTIVE PAUSE

How do you group your students? How could flexible grouping help you differentiate?

Content

One convergence point between flipping and differentiating instruction is content. In a flipped environment, you keep content intentional. In differentiated instruction, you change the content to meet students' needs. But in both approaches, content plays a key role in meeting students where they are in the learning process. We have our own approach to building tiered instruction within an in-class flip. When planning station or in-situ work, students' differences and needs become the main resource to plan. So, we guarantee different opportunities for students to engage with, apply, and absorb the content. We do this by involving the different thinking skills proposed in the revised

Bloom's taxonomy (shown in Figure 6.2). Students are always at different cognitive levels, even though they are in the same class. We can't ignore their differences and plan generically without our particular students in mind.

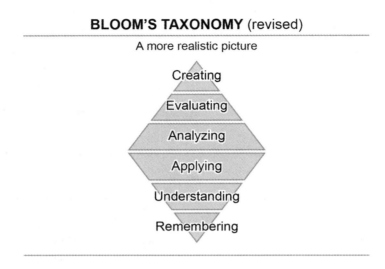

BLOOM'S TAXONOMY (revised)

A more realistic picture

Creating

Evaluating

Analyzing

Applying

Understanding

Remembering

Figure 6.2. Bloom's Taxonomy Diamond Form

Ms. Bauer, for example, is a social studies teacher at a high school in Brazil. She works in a bilingual school, and she teaches her subject in English. However, her twenty-four students are at different levels of readiness and skill in her classroom. Her school uses the Content and Language Integrated Learning (CLIL) method. CLIL helps students become familiar with the language they're learning in content class, as well as in English class. Ms. Bauer identified her students' levels by administering a diagnostic test at the beginning of the school year. So she knows exactly what her students struggle with in terms of language and content. Her students' needs and content gaps vary, but because she's aware of them, she is able to adapt instruction to everyone.

Of course, this doesn't mean that she plans twenty-four different lessons every day. But knowing her students' various levels helps Ms. Bauer cater to their needs. As Ms. Bauer planned her in-class flips, she built an in-class tutoring system for struggling students where student tutors assist during class activities. She also tiers instruction by preparing different stations according to Bloom's taxonomy. She has her class divided into six stations (one for each thinking skill). Each day, she invites students to pick the type of activity with which they feel most comfortable. However, she also invites them to go up the ladder and try something more difficult every time. Students in Ms. Bauer's class are autonomous and have learned the value of thinking about their own strengths and weaknesses.

For example, today she is teaching historical Latin American figures and their biographies. She prepared two vocabulary activities with readings assigned in the LOTS stations. For the HOTS stations, she thought of activities mediated by technology. She expects students to produce and create at the same time as they analyze information. Below, you can see a chart of Ms. Bauer's station plan. She contemplates Bloom's taxonomy levels in the planning of activities and resources and facilitates the tiering of instruction for all learners' levels (shown in Figure 6.3).

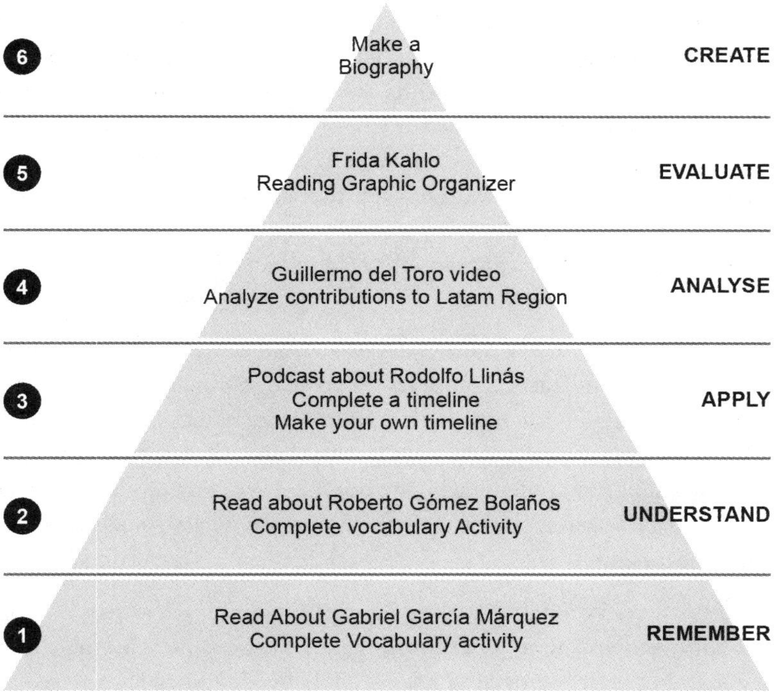

6	Make a Biography	**CREATE**
5	Frida Kahlo Reading Graphic Organizer	**EVALUATE**
4	Guillermo del Toro video Analyze contributions to Latam Region	**ANALYSE**
3	Podcast about Rodolfo Llinás Complete a timeline Make your own timeline	**APPLY**
2	Read about Roberto Gómez Bolaños Complete vocabulary Activity	**UNDERSTAND**
1	Read About Gabriel García Márquez Complete Vocabulary activity	**REMEMBER**

Figure 6.3. Station activities planned around Bloom's taxonomy.

By planning her activities around Bloom's taxonomy diamond, Ms. Bauer made sure to have both LOTS and HOTS activities. The level of difficulty increased during the lesson and students went as deep as possible in their learning. Also, by including a blend of digital and analog tools, she differentiated access and style, and diversified content for all students' preferences.

REFLECTIVE PAUSE

How can you use Bloom's taxonomy to choose or create content that fits your students' needs and levels?

Choice

Differentiation occurs when you provide choice to students through activities in the in-class flip. Using learning routes or paths that give students a sense of direction in their learning is one way to do so. Providing more than one learning option is another way. To achieve true student autonomy, students also must discover which option to choose, and we can guide them. Give students a sense of freedom by structuring the choices you offer them. You don't want to leave them lost among a sea of options. Choice management tools such as paths, learning menus, choice boards, and graphic organizers help us structure learning options. These tools display choices clearly and are not daunting to learners.

A learning route or path could be a checklist or a visual layout of the stations or class-work; you can also present learning options via an infographic or a mind map. Imagine the different routes students can take with certain content and offeri them a path. Offering a learning path is especially useful the first time you use the mixed station rotation configuration. For students who are not used to choosing their own steps to work on, suggesting a learning path shows them one way to start making their own decisions in their learning.

Holec defined learner autonomy as "taking charge of your own learning" (1981). Student autonomy requires more than learning paths to become achievable. Reflection after using a learning path is crucial to raise student awareness of the metacognitive process happening. Reflection helps guarantee that students understand that they are making decisions about their learning. Much like learning paths, learning menus and choice boards are tools that help clarify students' needs and preferences.

Carol Cummings proposes a menu of activities in her book *Winning Strategies for Classroom Management* (2000). She writes that choice is critical in helping students maintain their focus on a task, thanks to the exhilaration and inspiration that having a choice produces. A menu of activities, also known as a learning menu, offers students activity choices in the form of a restaurant menu. The activities follow a sequence in the same way menus generally do (e.g., appetizers, main dishes, desserts). Dessert almost always arrives last, for instance. Learners are provided with a learning menu to design their own "meal" combination (Carbaugh & Doubet, 2016). Students can choose the order and type of tasks with which they want to engage. The menu of activities helps mitigate time and task constraints (Cummings, 2000). Figure 6.4 provides a brief explanation of how the menu sections work.

Figure 6.4. A learning menu about learning menus.

Choice boards take into consideration student readiness and interest differences (Tomlinson, 2014). With a choice board, you present assignments in a chart or grid. In creating a choice board, think of the different levels students are at, and place activities accordingly in the chart. Students can then choose the activities that best fit their needs. You can design choice boards as a grid, a bingo game, or a Think-Tac-Toe. It is amazing to see how having learning choices motivates students.

Carolina has a problem in her class: students don't like to use the textbook (shhh—she doesn't like it either). So when she has to use it, she plans the lesson in the form of a choice board so students may decide on the activities they want to do. She includes all the activities in the two-page lesson from the textbook on a poster, and students do them at their own pace and in their own time. Normally, Carolina sets this up in the form of a Think-Tac-Toe (see the image below). She then gives cards to students, who draw their tic-tac-toe grid and mark their Xs and Os as they finish the activities. This is a fantastic way to modify a lesson to motivate students. Learners feel encouraged when asked to make their own decisions.

View Carolina's choice board for an academic writing class by scanning the QR code or visiting the URL: **bit.ly/3gAlfmX**

For more information on using these strategies to create student choice, see Chapter 6.

REFLECTIVE PAUSE

Which of the previously mentioned choice activities resonated more with you? How could you include more choice within your planning?

Feedback

Feedback is crucial in any type of teaching and learning environment. Feedback informs students about how they are doing and what steps they need to take to improve their learning. In the same way, student feedback gives valuable information to the teacher. George Couros, author of *The Innovator's Mindset* (2015), emphasizes the importance of asking for student feedback throughout the academic year so that students can enjoy your teaching changes within that same learning period. Timely feedback is the key to improvement for all.

Moreover, feedback ties into continuous teaching reflection, an indicator of the Professional Educator pillar as proposed by the FLN in 2014. Collecting student insight gives us a closer view into their thinking processes, interests, and specific needs. Robert Talbert (2017, p. 101), a higher education flipped learning expert, emphasizes that "getting regular feedback on students' learning experiences is especially important in a flipped learning environment to have actionable information about student perceptions of flipped learning and to snuff out potential problems before they snowball into serious issues." Regarding differentiated flipping, Carbaugh and Doubet (2016) emphasize the need to frequently collect information from students to provide timely feedback and address mistakes. Thus, in the student-centered class, student feedback has a vital role in optimizing the learning experience for all.

Finding time for appropriate feedback is challenging. Big classes and students at various levels challenge the teacher. So, varying feedback with the in-class flip can help you to reach all students in your classes. To collect feedback from students, we have used activities like exit slips, comments, written reflections, and oral feedback.

We have also provided feedback in different ways for all students. We give personalized feedback to students in-class, as a whole group, to pairs, one-on-one, digitally audio or video recorded, and even flipped (before class). We include feedback in our in-class flip lesson plans to collect student data and analyze it to think of instructional changes. Hence, this has become one of our starting points to differentiate how we teach.

It is true that asking for student feedback is not common in all teaching cultures and could be a challenge. We also know teachers may feel afraid of asking learners what they think about our teaching. Nobody wants to hear that something is not right, that what we are doing is boring or that they dislike our classes. But if we are trying to build a growth mindset, these honest comments become the basis for professional and personal growth and are part of an ongoing reflective process. When learners are at the center of our planning and decision-making processes, we learn what they need. If student feedback is honest and we are flexible to adjust our teaching with a growth mindset, we can only win.

REFLECTIVE PAUSE

How often do you ask students for feedback on your teaching? How can feedback inform differentiation in your classes?

Student Interventions

You can use in-class flipping to promote peer instruction and peer tutoring. Teachers can use students' different paces in understanding concepts to create a peer-instruction or peer-tutoring component in their class. Keep in mind that a learning culture is crucial for peer instruction and peer tutoring to work. Respect for each other is critical when students learn together. For these strategies to work, students have to feel empowered by each other and by the teacher.

Peer Tutoring

In peer tutoring, teachers identify students' strengths and weaknesses to assign roles. Students with a higher level of skill or readiness become the tutors; students who need to improve or who have difficulties understanding the material are the tutees. Tutor students must have a respectful attitude towards the tutee to guarantee a safe environment to learn. Also, the teacher should promote the idea of teaching as a learning approach. In this way, the tutors will see the value in teaching and won't feel "used." Both tutor and tutee must realize that they will be learning from each other. The teacher should clarify that she has made pedagogically sound decisions to shape the experience, and that she knows this technique will optimize the learning experience for both tutor and tutee.

Mr. Gonzalez is a Spanish teacher at a school in Australia. He realizes that his students struggle quite a lot with grammatical structures. The textbook he uses includes a lot of metalanguage (which confuses students). Following is his in-class flip roadmap.

- He embraces the in-class flip to ensure that every student will understand the concepts for the specific grammatical rule he teaches.

- He prepares a video lesson for the grammar point.

- He includes some questions and reflections to check students' understanding as they watch.

- He assigns the video for students to watch in pairs with their devices; they then answer the questions together.

- He pairs students according to results from previous grammar video accountability activities to guarantee every student understands the concepts. (Some students quickly understand the grammar points and easily do the exercise. Other students get most answers wrong.)

- He uses learner analytics available to him on the LMS to view student data and make the pairing-up decision.

- He prepares specific guiding questions for both students (tutor and tutee) to consider during the class session.

Students with a better grasp of grammar tutor, while students with difficulties are tutees. Both are expected to try to understand the grammar concepts presented and to do some activities. But their activities are different according to the level of skill of each. Mr. Gonzalez is careful in crafting activities where the tutor has to intervene in the tutee's process. Also, the tutee reflects on the role of the tutor in understanding the grammar point. After the activity, both students feel happy and accomplished because they had learned at their level.

REFLECTIVE PAUSE

Do you trust your students to be successful at peer tutoring or peer instruction? Why or why not?

Student support

What matters most in class is how teachers support students in their learning. Thus, when you have students who struggle in class, it is crucial for these students to know they can get the necessary support at the right time. The in-class flip allows the teacher to offer immediate support. For example, in a classroom where certain students need to review an explanation, they can access the flipped content in class. The presence of the teacher when students are accessing the flipped content permits just-in-time support to happen. If review material confuses students, they can reach out to the teacher and receive immediate support.

Timely Guidance

For students to apply learning strategies, the teacher needs to have the skill set to guide them. Teaching students to actively consume audio or video, take notes, revise content, and answer questions is important. Students who know how to perform these tasks are more likely to be successful. But in a regular flip, teachers may experience difficulties observing students at work. In an in-class flip, it's much easier.

Another example of timely guidance is when the teacher monitors while students work by themselves. The teacher can provide on-the-spot feedback to everybody on a misunderstood aspect. That way, the teacher remediates the situation instantly. This is different from providing whole group feedback in the next lesson.

Flipping keeps you focused on differentiation. You become more aware of student pace, learning preferences, struggles, and questions. You get the chance to have a constant conversation with each student, even if it's only for a minute or two during each class. Those moments become valuable time to connect with them and build stronger relationships. In our experience, the in-class flip gives us more time to get to know students.

TEACHING SPOTLIGHT

Katie Lanier is a physics teacher in Allen, Texas, U.S.A., who needed more "just in time" teaching moments, so she decided to give the in-class flip a try. During a second-year physics lesson, Katie's students were assigned a circuitry design project. Some students had enough background knowledge to move forward, while others needed more review. Providing review material at many levels allowed the students to learn what they needed to be successful. This removes the feeling of students being singled out for not knowing what they "should have already known." Meeting the students where they were in their level of understanding helped them all to reach the level necessary to do the task. Even those who overestimated their knowledge level felt comfortable enough to go back and review.

For Katie, the main benefits of in-class flipping include meeting needs in a timely manner, giving students the opportunity to ask questions while reviewing content, and immediately discussing the content to check for understanding.

Following are Katie's best practices for planning in-class flips:

- Create or find short videos that address questions and cover varied levels of a topic.

- Confirm that students are actively watching, taking notes, etc., and not just going through the motions.

- Don't limit video watching to class time. Some students will choose to watch at other times. Let them.

THE IN-CLASS FLIP AROUND THE WORLD

"My students were at varying levels of the curriculum, and our school had a focus on student well-being and anxiety. I found that the in-class flip provided a good strategy for my classes."
—Jeremy Cumming, Year 9–13 religious education teacher, Nelson, New Zealand

CHAPTER **7**

Planning an In-Class Flip

> **This chapter addresses several ISTE Standards:**
>
> **2.5. Designer**
> Educators design authentic, learner-driven activities and environments that recognize and accommodate learner variability. Educators:
>
> *a. Use technology to create, adapt, and personalize learning experiences that foster independent learning and accommodate learner differences and needs.*
>
> *b. Design authentic learning activities that align with content area standards and use digital tools and resources to maximize active, deep learning.*
>
> *c. Explore and apply instructional design principles to create innovative digital learning environments that engage and support learning.*
>
> **2.6. Facilitator**
> Educators facilitate learning with technology to support student achievement of the ISTE Standards for Students. Educators:
>
> *a. Foster a culture where students take ownership of their learning goals and outcomes in both independent and group settings.*

> b. *Manage the use of technology and student learning strategies in digital platforms, virtual environments, hands-on makerspaces, or in the field.*
>
> d. *Model and nurture creativity and creative expression to communicate ideas, knowledge, or connections.*

NOW THAT YOU'VE READ ABOUT DIFFERENT IN-CLASS FLIPPING configurations and explored many examples of in-class flipping strategies, let's plan a lesson using an in-class flip so you can start applying it in your classes right away The following steps (shown in Figure 7.1) break down the process..

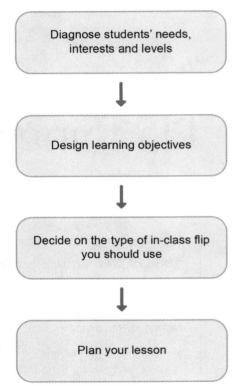

1. Diagnose Students' Needs, Interests, and Learning Levels

Every new term, we look forward to getting to know our students. Being aware of their strengths and weaknesses at the outset can really make a difference in our in-class flips, and in instruction in general. The first step in the implementation process for your in-class flip should be to diagnose students' needs, interests, and learning levels. You can assess this in a variety of ways:

Figure 7.1. The step-by-step.

- Ask students how they like to learn and what they dislike about learning in their classes. The answers will help you understand their learning preferences and select the activities and materials you plan to use.

- Carry out a formal diagnostic test where you prepare questions around the forthcoming curriculum.

- Design informal activities to collect feedback about students' level of readiness for the contents of your course.

• Design formative assessments that allow you to see how comfortable students are with the content for your course or the previous course. These activities can include interviews, presentations, a show and tell, an outing, etc. You may want to see how your students use the contents learned in real life.

• If you're able to do all of the above, you will have a comprehensive picture of your students' varying knowledge at the beginning of the term. This information will help you avoid cookie-cutter design in your instruction.

2. Design Learning Objectives

Many teachers view Bloom's taxonomy as a logical instructional framework for flipped learning. We use it constantly. Bloom's taxonomy allows us to focus on students' performance while remaining mindful of the different thinking skills we want them to develop. Consider having Bloom's taxonomy (Figure 7.2) at hand when lesson planning, and choose from it which skill(s) your students should develop during every lesson.

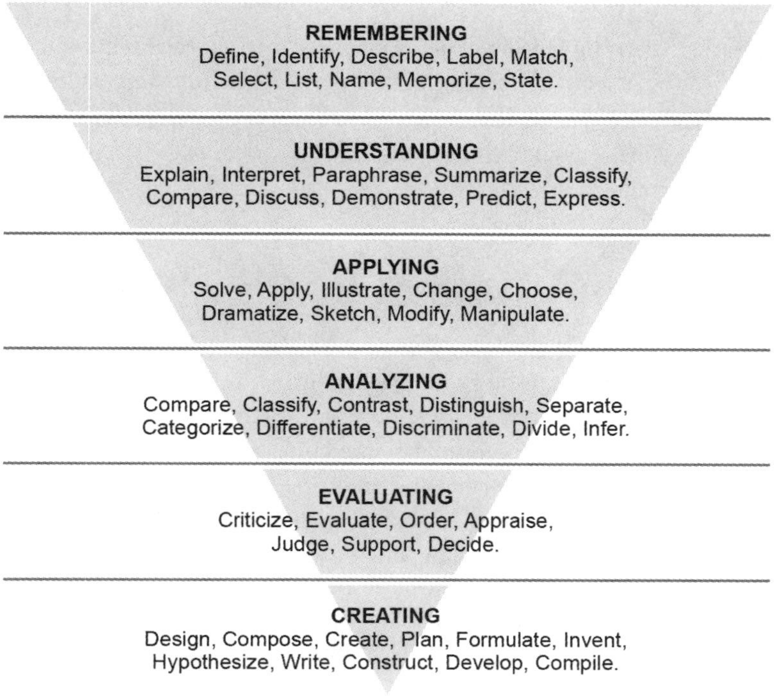

REMEMBERING
Define, Identify, Describe, Label, Match, Select, List, Name, Memorize, State.

UNDERSTANDING
Explain, Interpret, Paraphrase, Summarize, Classify, Compare, Discuss, Demonstrate, Predict, Express.

APPLYING
Solve, Apply, Illustrate, Change, Choose, Dramatize, Sketch, Modify, Manipulate.

ANALYZING
Compare, Classify, Contrast, Distinguish, Separate, Categorize, Differentiate, Discriminate, Divide, Infer.

EVALUATING
Criticize, Evaluate, Order, Appraise, Judge, Support, Decide.

CREATING
Design, Compose, Create, Plan, Formulate, Invent, Hypothesize, Write, Construct, Develop, Compile.

Figure 7.2. Bloom's taxonomy.

We suggest working through Bloom's taxonomy during your lesson planning to ensure your students are performing tasks at the different Bloom's levels in every class. Try to keep the objectives for the flipped content aimed at the "remember" and "understand" levels, and the learning objectives of the practice activities aimed at the higher-order thinking skills. This practice guarantees to maximize the depth of each student's learning. We find it effective to structure more meaningful learning during class time: we maximize our class time and achieve active learning in our classes.

When thinking of the learning objectives, most instructional design literature suggests considering different domains. For example, we encourage you to visit the Partnership for 21st-Century Learning framework, and the 4 Cs (Collaboration, Communication, Critical Thinking, and Creativity). This framework connects to the goals of UNESCO for learning in the digital age and considers aspects that traditional school ignores and that are pivotal for the workforce and the success of students in real life. Learn more by scanning the QR code or visiting the URL: **bit.ly/32vbSSn**

When thinking of objectives for your in-class flips, don't focus only on the content, but also on other soft skills students will develop through your lessons, such as teamwork, the ability to negotiate, and time-management skills.

Last but not least, learning objectives are not a mere instructional requirement. Inform your students of the objectives for the class, so they feel encouraged and empowered in their own learning. Knowing the objectives and the expectations for a certain lesson will empower students to own their learning process and to make decisions about it, a big step in learning autonomy.

3. Choose Your Type of In-Class Flip

After you have decided what your students need to learn—given their context, abilities, readiness level, and background knowledge—you are ready to choose your in-class flip configuration. Choosing an appropriate configuration is deeply rooted in the instructional objectives you have; it's all connected. Your lesson might involve introducing content or concepts, reviewing previous concepts, assessing a topic, or a hands-on workshop, as examples. Let's examine each lesson type in turn, since the choice for the type of in-class flip will depend on the type of lesson you want to plan.

Introducing Content or Concepts

If you want to teach a concept, process, or topic for the first time, you might use the sequenced and looped in-class flip configuration or the solo, duo, or group flip. During this type of lesson, students are expected to access the content on their own (since each one of them will have a different rate of learning). This model guarantees that the teacher is available to support students, expand concepts, clarify, and hand-hold. In a regular flip class, students access the content on their own outside the classroom, but the questions that may emerge must wait until the following class. On the other hand, if you set up the class as an in-class flip, students' questions will be answered on the spot.

Review Lesson

If your lesson will review previously acquired concepts, or clarify concepts before a test, you can use the sequenced, mixed, and looped station configurations or the solo, duo, or group flips. It all depends on how you plan to review the concepts.

If you select a sequenced configuration, you can plan your in-class flip so that students have to move up the ladder of knowledge by successfully performing an easy task before moving on to a more difficult task. This configuration can help you craft a mastery learning experience around a concept, topic, or idea. The level of complexity with which each student needs to work will help the teacher design a differentiated review.

In a mixed configuration, you may plan activities within the same level of difficulty, so regardless of the station they visit, students still review the required concepts. For instance, let's say students are learning how to multiply in a math class: you can have five stations focused on multiplying the same numbers. However, each station contains a different activity: a drawing task, a game, a quiz, matching, etc. The key is to aim for the same learning objective.

The way to differentiate your review in the mixed configuration will be according to the type of activity students perform (playing, matching, defining, classifying, categorizing, etc.).

With a looped configuration, you may plan activities within the lower tiers of Bloom's taxonomy, but you may also choose to plan some within the higher tiers, since students will have access to the flipped content via the flipped station.

The way to differentiate your review using this configuration is by paying extra attention to students whose learning of the topics may still be weak and who still need some confirmation of the concepts. They will feel safer just by having access to the content at the flipped station.

By selecting the duo or the group flip, a teacher may plan a lesson vertically to have students work cooperatively throughout the lesson while holding each other accountable for the learning of the different concepts as they navigate the activities. You might choose to plan the lesson either hierarchically (some tasks more important than others, thus, organized sequentially) or freely (all tasks equally important and left to the discretion of the students to decide what to do).

The way to differentiate your review with this configuration is by process. Students will work at their own pace, and the teacher can provide more personalized support.

Assessing a Topic

If you want to evaluate your students' mastery of a particular topic, you can execute your flip in a variety of ways.

Set up assessment stations. Each assessment station should offer a specific task allowing students to show mastery of content. As students work at the stations, circulate with a clipboard (as Cara Johnson does in her flipped mastery classrooms—see Chapter 13) and take notes of students' work by recording their difficulties, questions, and emerging topics to work on in upcoming lessons.

If you need to carry out individual assessments, you can include practice/review stations in the classroom and have students come to you one by one for an individual formal assessment, while the rest of the students are engaged in activities that will help them prepare for the formal assessment. For this situation, you can use any of the station rotation configurations. We suggest the mixed and the looped configurations, or you can use the half 'n' half station configuration in which half of the students practice activities while the other half get your direct feedback (see Chapter 5).

Hands-On Workshops

Sometimes a lesson is not about direct instruction but about practice using hands-on activities. If you teach a hands-on workshop using an in-class flip, you can use the sequenced or mixed configurations so planned activities can happen in an orderly fashion, and you can give students the most support possible. And your new setup still allows you to provide direct instruction for students who need to do the tasks in the session.

During a conversation with Jon Bergmann, global flipped learning expert, we learned about two ideas:

- Some science teachers use QR codes pointing to online videos showing the steps and instructions for lab experiments. Students then have the necessary information to complete the experiment.

- Some art teachers' classes use videos of drawing techniques so that students can watch them over and over before attempting the technique. Having access to the videos and to direct instruction (available in stations) helps ensure success.

TEACHING SPOTLIGHT

Antonio Bernabéu Pellús is a primary teacher at CEIP Campoazahar, a public school in Spain located in a rural area in Matanzas-Santomera (Murcia). He found the in-class flip to be a great way to get started in flipping a new course. Over a two- to three-week period, he trains students in actively watching videos and participating in his class activities. Once students clearly understand how to work with the videos and the course materials, Antonio then switches to a traditional flipped classroom.

Antonio also sees in-class flips as refreshers. He uses them when the content seems too complicated or when students are not doing their work as expected. For Antonio, the in-class flip is a fantastic strategy to prepare his traditionally-flipped class to work well.

4. Putting It All Together

Regardless of the flipping strategy you use, you should consider the following educational aspects, which will lead to a more complete and effective in-class flip. We have included a comprehensive checklist (Table 7.1) of these educational aspects, which you should consider throughout your planning phase.

TABLE 7.1
In-Class Flip Planning Checklist

EDUCATIONAL ASPECT	DESCRIPTION	✔
Objectives	Creating objectives for your class makes a significant difference. Here are some tips: Think about your objectives in terms of Bloom's taxonomy's verbs. Plan remembering and understanding tasks for the flip stations. Also, vary your tasks within the practice stations to include Applying, Analyzing, Evaluating, and Creating activities. If you are doing any of the in-situ (non-station) configurations, still consider Bloom's.	

(Continued from previous page)

TABLE 7.1

EDUCATIONAL ASPECT	DESCRIPTION	✔
Objectives *(Continued)*	Think your lesson backward and when designing the objectives, think of them as outcomes. What do you want your students to achieve by the end of the lesson? Then start thinking about the different steps you may need to prepare your students to take them wherever you want.	
Type of configuration	Think of which configuration best fits the needs of your lesson and your students. Station work: Sequenced, Mixed, Loop, Half 'n' half In-situ work: Solo, Duo, Group	
Warm up	To engage students in the content of the lesson, it is always a good idea to start with a fun activity that introduces the content they will be learning or that recaps information from previous classes. This is a way to connect students to the lesson and to motivate them. A warm-up can be a short game, hands-on activity, discussion, image exploration, etc.	
Flipped content: (what and how it will be accessed)	Key content is always in every lesson that students need to master. What is that key content and how will you flip it? Will it be curated, or will it be self-created?	
Flip accountability	Some type of accountability for the flipped content is crucial for teachers to know what a student's learning process is. By making learning visible, the teacher can assess and provide more accurate support for each student. Provide a specific focused task; this can be through a quiz (online or paper), comprehension activities, graphic organizer for note-taking, embedded questions (in a reading or video), worksheet, drawing, etc. This ensures that students are doing the work. (See Chapter 12 for accountability tech tools.)	

TABLE 7.1

Practice activities	An important question to ask is: how will our students apply the content learned? Whether through station or in-situ work, the activities planned should focus on higher order thinking, primarily, and fit within an active learning approach.	
Materials	There is nothing worse than having planned a great class and noticing in the middle of the activity that you forgot the tape, scissors, post-its, game counters, etc. One piece of material can change or even ruin a planned activity. Therefore, knowing exactly how many worksheets, laptops, markers, and other materials you need is crucial in the planning process. This goes hand in hand with how students are grouped so that you know the specific material needed for group, pair, and individual work.	
Timing	Estimate the amount of time each activity will take and then compare it to how long each activity took in the development of the lesson. This provides a record for future lessons in which the same types of activities will take place. Moreover, with in-class flips, it's a good idea to plan with the slowest-paced students in mind. For fast finishers, extra stations or anchor activities are helpful.	
Grouping	The way interaction will take place within your lesson should take an active role within the planning process. How you decide to group your students—whether they are working in pairs, in small groups, or as a whole class—should be thought through carefully. For ideas on how to group students flexibly, read about flexible grouping in Chapter 5.	
Assessments	Because assessment is an ongoing practice, it should be embedded within the activities of the lesson without leaving any gaps. Therefore, how we assess every activity in our lesson should be considered at the moment of thinking of the activity itself. It's good to ask questions such as: how will I ensure my students are understanding? Will I evaluate this or provide on the spot feedback? Will I assess individually? Will I pick anything to check later?	

(Continued from previous page)

TABLE 7.1		
EDUCATIONAL ASPECT	**DESCRIPTION**	✔
Wrap up (closure)	Every lesson should have a wrap up or closure of the lesson. This part is important for the students so they can have an overview of the material and the information can be organized in their minds. The closure of the lesson is oftentimes overlooked when our lesson time is running out. Nevertheless, it is as important as any other step since the last part will allow our learners to draw a final meaningful connection to what they learn.	
	The wrap up could be a summary or overview of the learning objectives and activities or a short assessment for a more precise idea of what needs to be reinforced. This will give insight into areas of confusion that learners still have and enable you to correct misunderstandings and fill in possible gaps learners still have.	
	Another way of wrapping up the lesson is by asking learners to share conclusions about what they learned or how they can apply the content in other contexts. You can also provide a preview of what is coming in the following lesson and its connection to what they just learned.	
	Some teachers provide or ask for student feedback as a way to wrap up the lesson, which is valuable and meaningful. However, as you will notice in the following section, you can both wrap up and include feedback. That way, your lesson becomes twice as meaningful.	

All the aspects described above will improve your teaching, whether you flip or not.

The Importance of Visualization When Planning an In-Class Flip

When planning an in-class flip, visualizing what will be done in the teaching setting is crucial for an effective development of the lesson. According to Scrivener (2005, p. 109), it is difficult for a teacher to fully predict how learners will respond to what has been planned; however, "the better prepared you are, the more likely it is that you will be ready to cope with whatever happens.". Therefore, planning increases the possibility of a more successful lesson. We recommend three ways to prepare depending on your lesson planning style and considering the various educational aspects mentioned above: sketchnoting, vertical or horizontal planning, and using lesson planning formats.

Sketchnoting

One way that you can visualize your lesson plan is by sketchnoting. Mike Rohde (2013) has defined sketchnoting as "Rich visual notes created from a mix of handwriting, drawings, hand-drawn typography, shapes, and visual elements such as arrows, boxes, and lines (p. 2)," so it's more than just taking notes. Sketchnoting combines text and visual elements, which are a perfect combination to visualize an in-class flip. Sketchnoting the layout of the classroom, particularly in the case of a station work flip, is a helpful and more accurate way to be sure all the elements of the lesson are being foreseen. It is helpful to include the type of classroom setting, seating arrangement, number of students, type of rotation, tasks, timing, and materials. Seeing it all on paper allows the teacher to notice if something is missing or hasn't been considered.

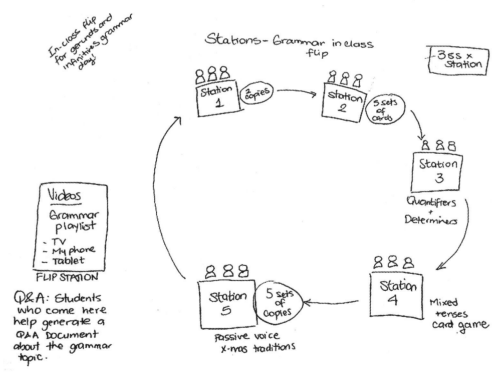

Figure 7.3. Sketchnote of an in-class flip.

In Figure 7.3, all the elements mentioned above have been included. Through the sketchnoting process, the teacher can make decisions to change arrangements, use various materials, or even document a Plan B if something unexpectedly goes wrong. Without a clear visualization of the logistics of the lesson, there may be missteps, and the lesson will not go as smoothly as expected.

You can see a video of lesson planning ideas by scanning the QR code or visiting the URL: **bit.ly/2MnzxwD.**

Vertical or Horizontal Planning

Another way to visualize your lesson involves writing your plan horizontally or vertically, depending on whether you have decided to do an in-class flip with stations or without them. If you are planning an in-situ in-class flip, then the ideal way to write your plan is vertically. In other words, vertically and in order, list the lesson activities one after the other to indicate the sequence of activities within the lesson.

On the other hand, if you are planning an in-class flip with stations, then horizontal planning (Tucker, 2016) is the best option. Here the term "horizontal" means that the activities are not necessarily sequenced chronologically, since students will work in different stations at the same time and doing various activities. The horizontal layout implies that activities are not locked into a specific order.

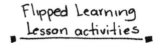

Figure 7.4. Vertical planning notes showing activities for a professional development lesson on flipped learning.

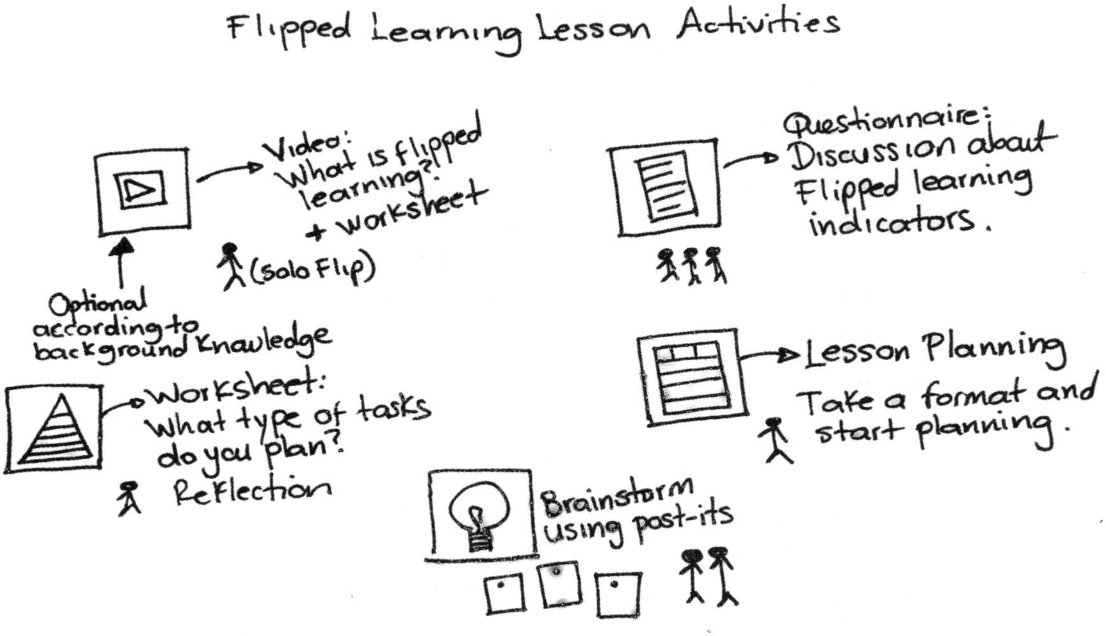

Flipped Learning Lesson Activities

Video:
What is flipped
learning?:
+ worksheet
(Solo Flip)

Optional
according to
background Knowledge

Worksheet:
What type of tasks
do you plan?
Reflection

Questionnaire:
Discussion about
Flipped learning
indicators.

Lesson Planning
Take a format and
start planning.

Brainstorm
using post-its

Figure 7.5. Horizontal planning notes showing
activities for a lesson on in-class flipping.

It is useful to keep a horizontal and a vertical view of the same lesson, because this allows the teacher to switch from an in-situ to a station work lesson easily, and vice versa. In Figures 7.4 and 7.5, you can see how the same lesson has been prepared for an in-situ and a station rotation flip. Notice how some activities have to be reconsidered when your strategy changes.

Planning with Formats

Even though teachers plan in many different ways, some teachers prefer to use a lesson planning format because it offers a ready-made order and layout for their planning process. Formats ensure all the elements to consider are included. In some cases, using a specific format is an institutional requirement.

TEACHING SPOTLIGHT

Steve Griffiths is a science teacher in Brisbane, Australia. He runs his whole year-nine science class as an in-class flip. He uses a learning management system and a self-made workbook that contains pre-video and post-video questions, exercises, and experiments. He also provides templates for writing Cornell notes for each video. His students work at their own pace. Steve monitors while interacting with every student in every lesson every day. Students do experiments at stations when they are ready. Each week, students take mastery quizzes that are self-marked. To view Steve's workbook, visit the URL: bit.ly/30k2ApH.

Following are some of Steve's top tips:

- Have the whole unit (videos and workbook) completed and available at the start of the unit to allow students to set their own pace.

- Schedule experiments over three or four lessons so students can complete them whenever they are ready.

- Provide spare headphones and tablets for students.

- Create a homework book providing students with a small amount of homework each week. Require parents (or guardians) to sign off each week.

- Spend time talking to every student; strive to know them and how they learn.

- Teach students how to watch the videos and take notes.

- Involve parents. The first week of homework asks each student to show their parents an introductory video.

- Have a seating plan for students.

- Ask students to help others

- Provide extension activities.

- Allow students to learn in ways other than viewing videos.

- Continuously reflect and improve.

CHAPTER 8

Planning Flipped Content for an In-Class Flip

> **This chapter addresses several ISTE Standards:**
>
> **2.5. Designer**
> Educators design authentic, learner-driven activities and environments that recognize and accommodate learner variability. Educators:
>
> a. *Use technology to create, adapt, and personalize learning experiences that foster independent learning and accommodate learner differences and needs.*
>
> b. *Design authentic learning activities that align with content area standards and use digital tools and resources to maximize active, deep learning.*
>
> c. *Explore and apply instructional design principles to create innovative digital learning environments that engage and support learning.*

REMEMBER THAT THE BENEFITS OF IN-CLASS FLIPPING ARE COUNTLESS, and that one of the most salient benefits is the ability to differentiate within your class through the content you create. When planning an in-class flip, include one of the strategies discussed below in the interest of offering the best possible experience for all learners.

Sketchnoting

Even though sketchnoting has been used primarily as a visual note-taking strategy, it can also be used as a flipped content resource that represents the content you want to teach in a unique way. With this strategy, you can condense an explanation, instruction, demonstration, etc. in one digital or physical page. Not to worry! You do not need to be an artist to sketchnote. Knowing how to draw the basic shapes (circle, square, triangle, rectangle, lines) will make up most figures one will need to explain a concept visually. Here are some steps to get started:

1. Create your own icon library of common objects you can doodle. A good alternative is to look for icons online and save them. You can use them as a model or even trace them.

2. In the planning phase, it is important to choose the content you want to flip and synthesize the key information you want to convey in the tool of your choice. A handy notebook or piece of paper will work. This can be with written notes, phrases, or bullet points.

3. Review the synthesized information and think visually. What information could be represented through icons or drawings?

4. Now review the leftover information that could not be easily converted into visual elements and decide what could be inserted into boxes and call-outs.

5. Decide on the layout of your sketchnote. Depending on the information you want to present, you can create a mind-map, a flow chart, a grid, a horizontal or vertical sketch, a process map, a path, or something original. Which one will convey your message best?

6. Put it all together. Make a first draft. Here you will probably find that you still have a lot of information or that your sketchnotes are taking up too much space, so this drafting stage is crucial because it will lead to pruning and synthesizing information even more. If you are drawing by hand, using a pencil and eraser is recommended as your sketchnote takes the shape you want it to. It is also in this step where you can assess the level of clarity of the information. Does it stand alone? If the student reads it, can they understand it without asking you?

7. When you feel satisfied with your draft, give it life! Add color, decorate, and enjoy the design process.

8. Finally, scan (if applicable) or make copies for students to use in class.

Figure 8.1 shows Martha's sketchnotes explaining the concept of flipped learning.

Figure 8.1. Sketchnotes about flipped learning used in in-class flips.

Infographics

The design of an infographic could easily follow the steps of the sketchnoting process with a much easier approach. Instead of an icon library, you need an images and digital icons library or go-to sources where you can find visual content. Make sure it is under a creative commons license, so you don't have any issues with copyright. You can always move elements around or use templates. The key to this type of resource is to find a balance between text and images as well as to decide on appropriate font size, style, and color palette. However, infographics also present loads of content in a synthesized way.

Learning Menus

To create a learning menu, you can prepare a 6x5 grid and include a variety of appetizers, main courses, desserts, and beverages (see explanation of learning menus in Chapter 6). We like to offer different tasks that share similarities at each level. Figure 8.2 is an example of a learning menu used for language learning which contains flipped content within some of the activities.

Appetizers (Choose two activities from this part of the chart)	Create a weekly vocabulary set on Quizlet.com	Play at least 1 weekly game in Phonetics Focus and bring screenshots to class	Join a conversation weekly in Voxopop or Voicethread and bring screenshots	Choose 1 weekly listening exercise from esl-lab.com and bring evidence	Join Duolingo and play weekly. Bring screenshots as evidence
Main Course (Choose minimum 3 of these activities)	Do grammar exercises in ego4u.com (grammar). Bring weekly evidence.	Make copies of "Grammar in Use" and do exercises. Bring weekly evidence to class.	Find a person to write to in English on Facebook or other platform and bring weekly evidence.	Write a journal in English and bring weekly pages.	Find a cultural exchange to attend (i.e. Cristine's project) and bring weekly evidence.
Dessert (Choose 1 of the activities in this chart)	Practice pronunciation using JenniferESL YouTube channel.	Record a weekly voice note and send to teacher via Whatsapp.	Practice pronunciation using The University of Iowa-Phonetics page. Keep record.	Watch a TV show in English (be it on TV or internet) and take notes of new words and expressions.	Record a weekly video and send to teacher via Whatsapp.
Hot drink (Extra bonus for extra practice)	Find a student with a lower level than yours and help them. +50 points	Practice your English with music using lyricstraining.com and perform. +50 points	Get a foreign boyfriend/girlfriend or friend to practice with Bring to class +100 points	Create a screencast to teach a language learning strategy to your peers +100 points	Go to a theater play, book reading or other event in English. Bring evidence. +100 points
Personalized activity					

Figure 8.2. Learning menu for showing mastery of different skills in an English class.

In Figure 8.2, the learning menu example, appetizers include easy and fun activities that involve low-order thinking skills. These activities simply engage students and have them practice a skill or two. The main course includes the tasks that invite them to create, evaluate, analyze, and apply (Bloom's higher-order thinking skills). Tasks are on the same tier of Bloom's taxonomy but the type of skill students will practice varies. Then desserts are similar to the appetizer in the level of difficulty of the tasks. However, these are also application tasks that invite students to create something. The hot drink is an extra bonus for extra practice. These activities take students out of their comfort zone. If your students are feeling extremely excited and creative about your class, you can have them create their own way of learning through the personalized activity.

As foreign language teachers, it is extremely difficult to offer authentic opportunities to practice language outside of class. Nonetheless, there are some places where students can do so. We use this "symbolic point system" in our learning menus to encourage our students to take their language learning up a nudge, but what we suggest is having students find examples of real-life applications of their classes. Can you do that with your class?

Now let's look at what a digital menu looks like when it is focused primarily on flipped content. Scan the QR code or visit the URL to see the digital version: **bit.ly/3tdAIDr**

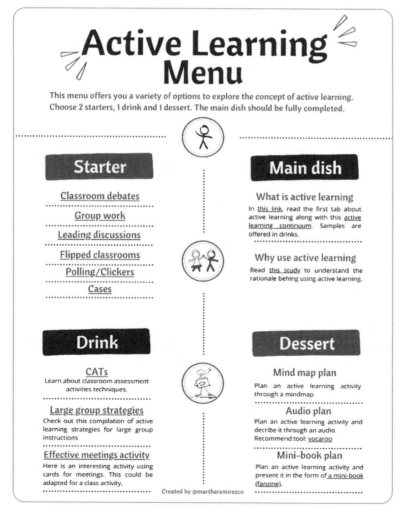

Figure 8.3. Digital learning menu about active learning.

As you can see in Figure 8.3, the menu has been used to teach about active learning, providing a variety of choices as well as a final task (dessert).

These activities only attempt to do one thing: have students use the content authentically in other scenarios different from class time. We know that the term in-class flip suggests everything only happens in the classroom, but we also think that autonomy clicks in students' minds when they think about our content all the time. How can you motivate your students to think about your class in other ways?

Choice Boards

Choice boards, which serve the same purpose as learning menus, could be presented to students in the form of a grid (as a Think-Tac-Toe or bingo). They are not aged bound or subject bound; therefore, they could be used for any purpose within a short-term or long-term class project.

Think-Tac-Toe

Creating a Think-Tac-Toe requires only nine activities. For those familiar with the game, it requires a simple 3 x 3 grid, which will be filled with the activities that students are expected to complete. You can also choose to leave the middle box as a free space for students to create their own activity that fits the overall objective behind the choice board. Since it's a tic-tac-toe, students should complete three activities of their choice that would lead to winning the game. In other words, the completion of the activities is put in parallel with what winning the game would imply.

Bingo

Creating a bingo choice board is more demanding since more choices are required. On this board, create a grid of 5 x 5, as in a common BINGO board. The BINGO replaces numbers (from the original game) with learning activities that students can decide to do to "win" the game. This means that twenty-four activities are available to learners in each square plus the free space in the center of the grid. With the dynamic of the game in mind, learners could do several tasks. For instance, they could complete a line composed of five activities in whichever order and direction they would like. If their choice includes the free space, then they would only have to complete four activities unless they are asked to create their own activity to fill in the free space square. The criteria for a win such as a vertical or horizontal line should primarily rely on the learners. Teachers can also ask students to complete the full board but since the goal is to provide choice, then it's a good idea to leave blank spaces within the board for students to choose the activities they will include or to leave this last option as a bonus (which students choose to do).

Scan the QR code to see a choice board Carolina designed for a professional development session with teachers. Feel free to make a copy and use it! **(bit.ly/3MR0S6O)**

Scan the QR code to see a digital choice board made by Martha for her advanced English class. Feel free to use it as well. **(bit.ly/3JeyljL)**

Flipping Instructions for Students

After almost two years of online teaching, we discovered what we have considered one of our best practices in flipping content: flipping instructions. Something as simple as writing down or recording instructions instead of providing them with direct instruction has shown significant change in class dynamics, student engagement, and differentiation, not to mention having stopped repeating ourselves to tell students what they had to do in an activity or task. We had not noticed how many times we repeated instructions until we had no need to anymore.

As student variances became more evident in online settings due to connection issues, access to certain resources, and technological knowledge, among others, the need to take instructions even further arose. Therefore, Martha designed instructions that combined Bondie and Zusho's (2018) differentiated "Inclusive Directions" approach with flipped learning (Figure 8.4). The inclusion of differentiation gave way to more rigor in the planning process and better learning outcomes. Thus, the concept of

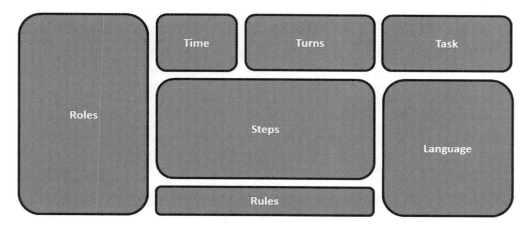

Figure 8.4. Elements of flipped differentiated instructions.

differentiated flipped instructions was born. As a result, the instructions are provided to students in a flipped format they can access that include the elements of turns, roles, rules, and time (Bondie & Zusho, 2018) along with steps, language, and a task (Ramirez, 2021).

 In her blog post, Martha shares a step-by-step explanation of how to plan these instructions with examples of different types of activities. Scan the QR code or visit the URL **(bit.ly/3w7Kmt0)** to start planning your instructions!

Learning Path or Route

Learning paths can be used with different aims. In a face-to-face classroom setting, this resource can be used in a station in-class flip for students to choose where they need to go based on their knowledge and understanding of the topic. By the end of the lesson, the path reveals which route they should take to reach their learning goals.

This strategy consists of asking students to identify within the path what stations or activities they want to study. Moreover, the teacher could also suggest a path, taking into account students' abilities to fulfill the tasks, whether they are lower- or higher-order thinking skills. This becomes visually helpful for the teachers since it allows them to see where the students are, what their needs are, and where they need to go. As the lesson progresses, the teacher can also have an idea of how fast or how slow students are completing their routes.

Another benefit of incorporating paths in the lesson is that students get a sense of organization, especially when the in-class flip brings a type of chaos as a side effect of the inclusion of choice. Our experience tells us that it is sometimes more difficult for students to accept a different and unfamiliar type of organization as opposed to teachers who are embracing a new teaching approach. When students understand that they are given choice and that they are the ones responsible for tracing their own learning path in a lesson, then the sense of disorganization becomes secondary.

Figure 8.5 shows an example of how a path could be provided to students.

In an online setting, learning paths can be used for in-situ in-class flips using digital tools that allow the student to click and decide what to do or to click and follow a sequence.

Figure 8.6 shows a decision-making path Martha designed to teach about perspective and stance in an in-situ solo in-class flip. This path was designed using a slides tool and students were expected to complete it before returning to the main room with all

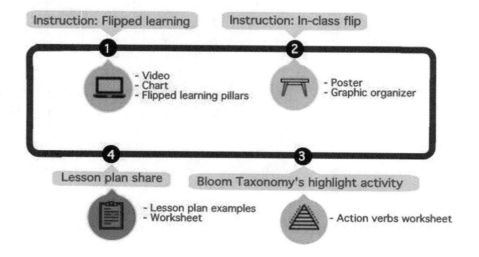

Figure 8.5. Path for a loop configuration in a teacher training session.

classmates to present their perspective and stance. This example shows four moments of choice: in the first slide, students choose a door to go through which will take them to the perspective they will have to take (psychological, environmental, scientific, etc.); then, students move on to the issues slide and choose an issue they prefer; next, they choose a drawer that will tell them what their stance is (in favor or against); and finally, they will choose the vocabulary and expression they want to use to defend their stance.

Carolina is known for creating didactic sequence paths. Figure 8.7 is an example of an in-class flip about data collection methods and instruments. Here students must click on each book to access the instructions and flipped explanations of the content as Carolina monitors and provides support.

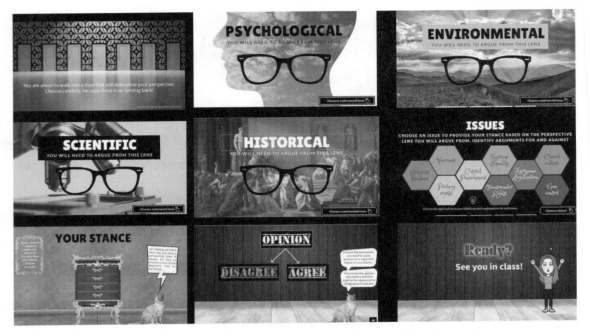

Figure 8.6. Digital decision-making learning path about perspective and stance

HyperDocs

We're providing a brief overview of how we create our own HyperDocs. You can even go to one of our samples, if you scan the QR code or visit the URL: **bit.ly/3h7PZwE.**

HyperDoc structure

Even though multiple templates and instructional approaches to HyperDocs exist, we chose the structure Lisa, Kelly, and Sarah created: Engage, Explore, Explain, Apply, Share, Reflect, and Extend in our classes.

Engage   This section is the hook of your HyperDoc. With an amazing hook, students become interested in the topic and hopeful for the learning that is about to happen (Burgess, 2012). Think of something that will engage your students in the content you are about to share with them. You can choose whatever makes you and your students comfortable: a joke, a story, a meme, a video, a song, a video, etc. What matters is that you engage learners with the content and invite them to click further.

Figure 8.7. Digital didactic sequence path for a research lesson.

Explore   In this stage of the HyperDoc you give students resources to get acquainted with the topic at their own pace. Lisa, Kelly, and Sarah suggest creating "multimedia sets" that are charts full of carefully selected links for students to explore. The beauty of this technology is so powerful, we can offer links to simple tools like texts and videos, but also to more elaborate ones as museum tours (via Google Earth). The purpose of the explore section of your HyperDoc is to have students navigate the topic on their own and feel empowered to learn by themselves with your guidance and expertise in the curation of content.

Explain   In this stage of the HyperDoc, apply direct instruction magic with the help of other technologies or materials. In this section, you provide links for students to access text materials, posters, podcasts or videos for them to learn about the topic (see Chapter 12 on technology to be used for ideas on how to modify your materials). If you are thinking of a duo flip, you can implement the peer-instruction strategy and have students first watch the explanation of the material you have prepared individually, and then follow Mazur's ideas and add a bit of peer-instruction to your instructions in the HyperDoc. Students then explain the content to one another. As you are free to respond to questions and to monitor, you can be certain mistakes are not made and no content inaccuracies are being transmitted by students.

Apply   After you have managed to interest students, and they have received the more formal explanation of the topic, they are ready to apply the content. So here is where you let your hair down and go creative in crafting practice activities for students to show they have understood the topic and they can use it in real life. Drilling exercises, composition writing, problems, experiments, simulations, case-studies, matching exercises, etc. are just a few activities you could design / curate for your students. This stage also lends itself to a duo flip since students can apply knowledge collaboratively and learn together as they apply content to real-life tasks together. As you create your HyperDoc, you can add instructions for students to turn to their classmate face-to-face and talk about something or to solve a problem together.

Share When students apply what they've learned through the previous stages in the HyperDoc, they are ready to share, to take learning outside of their heads and collaborate. Thus, using collaborative websites, and including cooperative face-to-face learning activities can enhance the learning experience and give students the chance to show their learning to someone different than the teacher. We like to foster sharing outside students' comfort zone and going global with the use of Twitter, Facebook, and other social media websites. However, when working on a HyperDoc in the classroom, we foster sharing through the use of some of Kagan's cooperative learning structures (Round Robin, Four Corners, Think-Pair-Share, etc.)

Reflect Once students work with the information and apply it, it is time for metacognition to take over. They can either reflect about the HyperDoc itself and their performance and take in it. Or they can provide feedback to the teacher in making HyperDocs better for the future. We like to foster both. For us, teacher feedback on student work is equally important to student feedback on teacher work, we believe that both (teachers and students) learn equally in every class session. We normally use wall websites like Padlet to collect student feedback, but you can integrate other tools like email, Adobe Spark, even WhatsApp messages; what's really important is to promote reflection.

Extend If you were thinking of those fast finishers, or maybe of the importance to promote further thinking and engagement with the topics, the extend stage in the HyperDoc invites you to look for additional resources with which you can help students extend the learning experience.

Although HyperDocs are initially an online tool connected to Google and its apps, they don't have to be. One of the biggest gains in using HyperDocs for our in-class flips has been the development of student autonomy and mastery learning. Students can move at their own pace with a HyperDoc, and if you plan it well with only one class session, you can have all your learners engaged with the content while you provide assistance and facilitate learning on the spot. Figure 8.8 shows you HyperDocs in a nutshell.

Engage

To **engage** students at the beginning of a lesson, insert video, image, quote, or another inspirational hook in this box.

Explore

Curate a collection of resources (articles, videos, infographics, text excerpts, etc.) for students to **explore** a topic.

Explain

Use this section of the HyperDoc to **explain** the lesson objective through direct instruction using your favorite web tool, or gather students together to teach the content.

Apply

Create an assignment for students to **apply** what they learn by using web tools to create, collaborate, and/or connect beyond the classroom.

Share

Collect student work to provide feedback, and/or include a section for students to **share** work with an authentic audience.

Reflect

Include an opportunity for face-to-face or digital **reflection** to guide students along their learning progression and set new goals.

Extend

Add links to more activities and online resources to **extend** the learning.

Figure 8.8. HyperDocs Template from HyperDoc.co

No Technology

We say HyperDocs are one way to do the solo, duo, or group flip because you just have to create the HyperDoc and take students to a computer lab and let the magic happen. However, you may craft the same learning experience in a classroom without technology by thinking of the same instructional steps and providing more analog materials to students. Even if you have no 1:1 technology and you only have one presentation station and a couple of devices in your classroom, you can create a learning experience that follows the steps of a HyperDoc and guarantees a deep learning experience for all.

Planning is for us the secret recipe for successful in-class flips. As teachers, we always plan our lessons but sometimes we "go with the flow." When teachers carefully plan an in-class flip, they create a fruitful learning experience for learners. However, there is no one-size-fits-all planning template. We hope that some of the options in this chapter combined with your teaching style allow you to integrate in-class flipping into your teaching toolkit.

REFLECTIVE PAUSE

What do you predict might be your own challenges when planning an in-class flip lesson?

THE IN-CLASS FLIP AROUND THE WORLD

"One tool that I have used to differentiate during my in-class flip is the HyperDoc. A HyperDoc is an interactive way to deliver instruction to our students. It is student-centered and guides the learner through a lesson, increasing in depth while working at their own pace. The HyperDoc is the perfect complement to in-class flipping. Students work on the HyperDoc in class, while freeing up the teacher to move about the room doing formative assessments or pulling small groups. The HyperDoc lends itself to natural differentiation. They HyperDoc makes it easier to provide a variety of opportunities for learning, processing, and assessing the lesson. By incorporating the 4Cs into the lesson, my classroom is robust in collaboration, critical thinking, creativity, and communication." —Susan White, sixth-grade math teacher and MS Math Technology Coach, Creekside Middle School, Woodstock, Illinois, U.S.A.

CHAPTER 9

Ten Tips for Getting Started

THE IN-CLASS FLIP IS A HIGHLY EFFECTIVE MODEL once you get the hang of it, but it may take you a while to feel fully confident in implementing it. We have gone through the experience many times and have discovered the best ways to avoid roadblocks. We want to help you avoid making the same mistakes we made. Following are some tips to help make your implementation of the in-class flip smooth.

1. Visualize

There can be many moving parts in an in-class flip. It is important to have a clear mental picture of where these parts are placed and how they work during the flip. Maybe you are like Martha, who can see paths and settings easily and can design cool e-diagrams of pretty much everything. Or maybe you are more like Carolina, who has a hard time picturing concepts, so she has to talk them over and then attempt to draw them on paper. Regardless of your thinking style, devise a way to visualize how your in-class flip will happen. Draw a map of your classroom with the location of (as an example) chairs and tables, the board, and a presentation station (smart board, television, projector, etc.), and think about what the role of each element would be during class time. Drawing your classroom map will help you understand what you need to do before the in-class flip session and will help you be prepared.

There are other aspects of the in-class flip that you should envision. It's important to think about the kinds of materials students will use (papers, pens, pencils, books, eBooks, apps, websites, electronic devices, earphones, calculators, etc.) and how you will distribute these materials to students (boxes, envelopes, paper bags, gift wrap, online platform, a link, digitally via QR code, etc.).

Consider how you will group students for each activity (individual work, pair work, group work, station work, etc.). We understand it might seem daunting to consider all these aspects, because we felt that way ourselves, but Martha designed an in-class flip layout (accessible by scanning the QR code or visiting **bit.ly/2vFUbP7**) to facilitate this visualization process for you.

You may want to use this layout the first time you visualize your own in-class flip, and then design your own layout as you gain experience.

2. Plan Your Lesson Carefully

Even though lesson planning is usually second nature for teachers, when doing an in-class flip it is pivotal to do a more detailed and thorough plan, because there are many variables to consider. Be ready to think about the following aspects when planning your in-class flip.

Content

Remember that in this form of flipped learning, the delivery of content and practice coexist in the same physical space. You, the teacher, do not deliver the content. In the in-class flip, you will design and assign content for students to access individually (or in pairs or groups), but within the classroom. When thinking about your lesson plan it's important to review your content and think of the most effective way to deliver it to students (videos, podcasts, packets, slides, etc.).

You should in-class flip using your most complex content. Complex content will likely require more support from you, and the configurations of in-class flipping facilitate your interaction with students in different ways and at different stages of the learning process.

Practice Activities

These activities are the core of your lesson, so you need to be careful when planning them so that students' needs and preferences are met (see Chapter 6 for more on differentiation). We use Bloom's taxonomy to design practice activities. We balance low and high order thinking skills in every activity so students can fully develop their potential.

Time

During an in-class flip your perception of time will likely change. You will not be in front of the classroom lecturing, so all (or most) of your time can be made available to students.

For your students, time can be an asset or a liability depending on how you plan for it. Using timers and setting time limits for tasks will help students stay focused.

Stations and Rotations

If you are using one of the four station configurations, think about the stations and the rotations. When planning stations, think about their purpose and how helpful they are for students to achieve the learning goals for the session. Also think about aspects such as station size, organization, materials for each station, outcomes, and assessment.

Student Grouping

In an in-class flip you will maximize student-to-student interaction, so group them purposefully. You can group students by proficiency level, learning styles, learning needs, or interests.

Once you have a thorough plan ideation for your in-class flip, it will run much more smoothly.

3. Embrace the Chaos

Some teachers avoid chaotic classes. During an in-class flip chaos is a benefit, because post-chaos, deeper learning is the payoff. During your in-class flips, especially your first attempts, the class can seem out of control. The organization of chairs into stations, posting materials on the wall of the classroom, setting up the tubs with the lab materials, cutting pieces of paper, deciding how many students do what first, setting timers—all of this can create a crazy atmosphere. But once you and your students master flipping, your need for control will wane. Normally, the idea of chaos seems opposed to a fixed concept of discipline where students are expected to be quiet and organized. In an in-class flip, students have the opportunity to move around, be creative, and demonstrate their learning, which in the long run contributes to a more personal concept of discipline.

4. Keep Slower-Paced Students in Mind

One of the main benefits of the in-class flip is the ability to differentiate learning. As you plan your in-class flip, slower-paced students will benefit from having tiered activities. It is important to give all students the message that it is not necessary to finish fast but to work through activities thoroughly and to understand deeply. You can add a "fast finishers" station to make sure the slower-paced students are not rushed to finish.

A fast finishers station aids differentiation in many ways. First, it removes the pressure from slower-paced students. Second, it shows fast finishers that all students deserve respect for their individual abilities. And third, it provides fast finishers with fun, challenging, and higher-level tasks to help them grow at their fast pace.

5. Start Slowly

In-class flipping involves a lot of planning (as you may already suspect). Attempting to in-class flip every class session would only burn you and your students out. In-class flips brings novelty into the classroom, but if you overdo it, the novelty aspect will wane. So, start slow. Plan your first in-class flip thoroughly and learn from your own mistakes. Every time you do it, you will do it better, but do not force yourself to do it more than you're comfortable with.

6. In-Class Flip the Most Complex Content

Since the in-class flip helps you to differentiate and be by the side of students through-out the entire lesson, consider reserving this mode of flipping for your most complex content. Revise your syllabus, find the topics that cause students to struggle, and in-class flip them.

7. Keep Instructions Super Simple (KISS)

Chaos is fine; confusion is not. When creating the instructions for your in-class flip, walk in your students' shoes and think as they would. Simplify. Enhance your instructions with models, drawings, figures, etc. to increase their clarity.

When working in stations, make sure your instructions are available on the wall or at every station. When working in in-situ (non-station) configurations, make the instructions centrally available, or give each student a copy. The simplicity, clarity, and readability of your instructions will determine the success of your in-class flip.

8. Get Feedback from Students

An important part of being a professional educator is to become a reflective practitioner. Your class might not always go as expected, and it's important for you to be flexible and constantly seek improvement.

A great way to find out how you are doing and how your in-class flip is being received by students is to ask them directly. You can ask students to fill out a simple exit survey, or you could use a website to collect students' impressions at the end of the class. In your students' perceptions you will find valuable insights that will help you shape your practice and refine your instructional design.

9. Get Feedback from Colleagues

Since sharing, collaboration, and reflection are desired characteristics of a flipped learning professional educator, feedback from colleagues is also essential. Working alone on your lessons will only get you so far. Including the objectivity and experience of colleagues will offer new insights. Do not hesitate to share your lessons and discuss issues with fellow educators. This practice will contribute to your educational and personal growth.

10. Always Have a Plan B

Having a Plan B is ideal for any teacher, but for an in-class flipper, it is a must. For example, when you prepare an in-class flip with devices, you will often have someone who forgot their headphones or whose headphones decided to stop working just before the activity—so always have a spare pair. Jon Bergmann, flipped learning guru, shared an interesting story of resourcefulness:

> I was on a plane when I was first flipping, and I saw that the plane threw out all the headphones after the flights. I asked the flight attendant if I could have them and explained that I was a teacher. She then came to me with a full bag of brand new headsets, and I got them for free. They were cheap, but they lasted a long time.

This example is just one of the many instances that might demand your creativity. We hope you see our point. Tap into your resourcefulness and find ways to solve any problems that may emerge when you in-class flip.

We hope these tips will help you get started with your in-class flips. We hope to spare you some frustration!

10

Accountability Measures

This chapter addresses several ISTE Standards:

2.6. Facilitator
Educators facilitate learning with technology to support student achievement of the ISTE Standards for Students. Educators:

c. *Create learning opportunities that challenge students to use a design process and computational thinking to innovate and solve problems.*

2.7. Analyst
Educators understand and use data to drive their instruction and support students in achieving their learning goals. Educators:

a. *Provide alternative ways for students to demonstrate competency and reflect on their learning using technology.*

b. *Use technology to design and implement a variety of formative and summative assessments that accommodate learner needs, provide timely feedback to students, and inform instruction.*

c. *Use assessment data to guide progress and communicate with students, parents, and education stakeholders to build student self-direction.*

Although you are often monitoring students' work during each in-class flip, it won't always be necessary. Students access the content within the classroom, yet what happens in their minds is not fully accessible to us. Do they understand the content you provide? Without some kind of accountability, it's hard to know. Keep accountability in mind by designing activities that lead to deeper learning.

We have identified some effective ways of including accountability at every stage in our classes. Following are some of our favorites.

Immediate Response Systems

If technology is available to you, you can use immediate response systems like Kahoot!, Socrative, or Plickers to ensure students are understanding content. We add one of these activities at the end of an input activity to quiz students before moving on to another activity. For example, in a station rotation, we can add a Kahoot! quiz for students to prove whether they fully understood the content. If they get all the questions right, then they can go on to the following station. Also, you can use it as a debriefing exercise. We have used this type of quiz at the beginning and the end of a class period to measure learning.

Sketchnoting or Note-taking

Sketchnoting and regular note taking are fantastic for holding students accountable for their learning. Earlier in our careers, we found that students would often take superficial notes, so we started exploring different ways to take notes. This is how we discovered sketchnoting as presented by @sylviaduckworth.

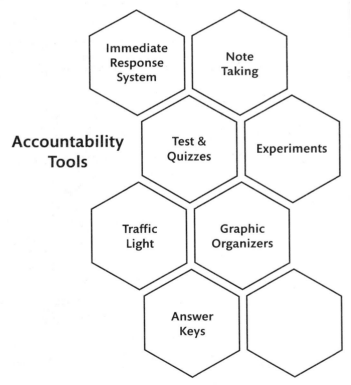

Figure 10.1. Accountability tools.

Figure 10.2. Sketchnote of the future tenses by Angi Perez and Mafe Salgado.

Sketchnotes have become an incredible learning tool for students! Using a combination of letters, symbols, and drawings (if students feel adventurous), note-taking becomes an active, engaging process. Within a station rotation plan, we ask students to use sketchnotes as a strategy to either consume content or to take notes from other resources such as videos or readings. They can do it as an individual task or as a collaborative one, where multiple students work together to create a single sketchnote.

For more ideas on how to use this strategy, look at the various examples Martha provides in her blog post about using sketchnotes for active learning. Scan the QR code or visit **bit.ly/33z5vOI**.

Testing or Quizzing

We often include a test or a quiz at the end of our lessons in the interest of getting students to see how much they have learned about a topic. You may find that in an in-class flip classroom culture, the emotional load of tests and quizzes diminishes. Students may still feel some pressure before a test, but we find they often start to take tests and quizzes with a more relaxed attitude since they now take them right after engaging deeply with content within the in-class flip.

Experiments

In science classes, experiments can be an excellent measure of accountability. Students might need to identify certain elements necessary for an experiment or follow the steps in a testing process. By creating an experiment within an in-class flip, teachers can see if students are mastering the material.

Traffic Light Accountability

We struggled to name this activity, but we hope the reference to a traffic light is international enough for you to imagine what we mean. We want students not only to understand the content they are tackling, but to show mastery. So we thought of a colorful way to represent understanding of the content by using the colors in a traffic light: red means "stop and review," yellow means "get ready to move on but keep reviewing," and green means "you are ready, go to the next topic."

You can create a simple chart with students' names and the number of activities in your in-class flip. Then, you add a colored dot sticker or use colored markers to fill in the chart. When students feel they have mastered a topic, they go to you. Once they've spoken with you (in an informal mastery check), you choose the color of sticker they deserve. Green means move to a new station or activity; yellow or red means stay at the current station to gain more skills. This simple, visual way to show mastery of a topic is effective for students.

Graphic Organizers

Graphic organizers are good learning tools for students and an assessment source for teachers. Graphic organizers are a way to make thought processes visible as well as for

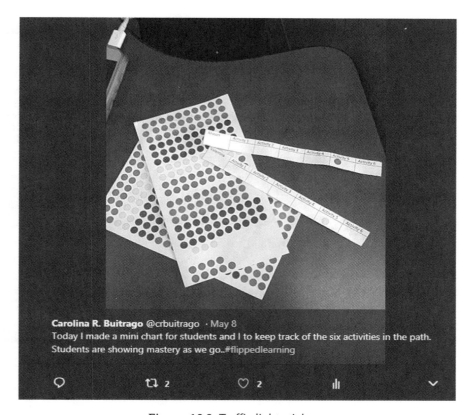

Carolina R. Buitrago @crbuitrago · May 8
Today I made a mini chart for students and I to keep track of the six activities in the path. Students are showing mastery as we go..#flippedlearning

Figure 10.3. Traffic light stickers.

students to organize their ideas to understand a topic better. Also, as students create their graphic organizers, they tend to think in a more structured way.

Answer Keys

Creating answer keys for activities is on our best practices list. Students can check their work as they complete the assigned tasks. This helps them develop autonomy, and it allows the teacher to get a better idea of students' understanding.

Whether you check accountability through a test, a quiz, a graphic organizer, or an experiment, it is important to offer activities that will hold your students accountable for their learning.

REFLECTIVE PAUSE

Which one of these accountability measures do you think is the most useful?

THE IN-CLASS FLIP AROUND THE WORLD

"I can help when my students need me. I do in-flip with more difficult concepts."
—Joanne Ward, math, Taipei, Taiwan

"Students are engaged. [It's] controlled chaos."
—Daniel Lumsden, K–12 math and accounting, St. Michael's College School, Toronto, Ontario, Canada

Overcoming Common Problems

d. Demonstrate cultural competency when communicating with students, parents, and colleagues and interact with them as co-collaborators in student learning.

2.5. Designer

Educators design authentic, learner-driven activities and environments that recognize and accommodate learner variability. Educators:

a. Use technology to create, adapt, and personalize learning experiences that foster independent learning and accommodate learner differences and needs.

b. Design authentic learning activities that align with content area standards and use digital tools and resources to maximize active, deep learning.

c. Explore and apply instructional design principles to create innovative digital learning environments that engage and support learning

WHEN LAUNCHING A NEW PEDAGOGICAL STRATEGY, you will always face some difficulties. Sometimes, such as with the traditional flip, it is student or parent buy in. Other times, such as with in-class flips, the obstacles that emerge are often in teachers' minds. Some teachers feel discomfort when a new mindset is expected, and they decide to stay on the safe side. Yet when teachers are willing to step out of their comfort zone, the advances in student engagement and learning will soon convince them that they made the right decision. In the following section, we explore two of the main obstacles that teachers encounter when implementing in-class flips. We will also outline ways to overcome these obstacles and succeed.

Challenges in Teacher Mindsets

The first category of obstacles is what Simon Borg (2009) calls "teacher cognition." It refers to what teachers (and administrators) think, know, and believe about themselves and education. Teachers' beliefs are powerful, because they determine teachers' decisions about their students' learning. We have identified five main mindset challenges within this category.

Mindset Challenge 1: Resistance to Innovative Practices

With in-class flips, you might encounter some resistance, as is often the case when introducing an innovative practice. This resistance might come from the administration or your colleagues. Criticism or skepticism often comes from school administrators. Some administrators see change and "chaos" as unacceptable. So you may have to break down some resistance.

How can you face resistance from others?

- **Take on the resistance.** Fight it. You may not *want* to have arguments during staff meetings, but a couple may well be worth it. With in-class flips you will be doing ground-breaking work. Stick to your ideals and find the courage to defend them. After all, you are not doing anything wrong, and in-class flips will yield results that will make colleagues and administrators take notice.

- **Share your teaching experiences and lessons.** Seeing is believing, and the best way to convince your peers that something works is to show it to them. Invite your colleagues to observe one of your flipped lessons, or take pictures and show them how it works. One way we countered resistance was by creating our blogs to share our teaching experiences and practices. We also invited colleagues to come into our classrooms and see it for themselves. This helped more than one of our colleagues and administrators to embrace the idea of in-class flipping and try it themselves.

- **Involve administrators and parents.** You can plan an in-class flip about in-class flips, and invite your school administrators to see how it works. You can also do an in-class flip for an open house day or parents' meeting to show parents how their kids will be working in your classroom. Parents are good advocates for teachers if they are happy with their kids' learning.

Mindset Challenge 2: Teachers' Definition of Discipline

Teachers often view discipline as the ability of students to sit still and quiet for the whole class period. This conception can become a teaching obstacle. Students are active and curious. They are discovering new things in the world all the time. Yet, the traditional educational paradigm forces them to adopt a set of behaviors that adults consider appropriate, even though they go against learners' nature. A passive learning environment becomes synonymous with a disciplined class, leaving no space for active learning to take place.

How can you overcome this flawed view of discipline?

- **Promote and develop a flexible environment in your classroom.** In flipped learning, the class environment should be flexible (FLN, 2014, para. 1). This means that teachers should modify classroom spaces so that students may access content and practice in different settings. In-class flip configurations create flexibility in your class environment and promote active learning. Because students have specific tasks to perform, they often get laser focused and use time better. You will be surprised at how quiet a classroom can get when students are actively learning. However, be prepared for a noisy class too. Noise levels will vary depending on the types of tasks you have set for your students.

- **Embrace temporary chaos.** One reason teachers refrain from trying an in-class flip is often the noise and mess that can result. However, this chaos is temporary, and it is a direct consequence of active learning. Once students focus on their tasks, the noise and mess become secondary to the deep learning that flips offer. A dread of messiness is about love of control, and in-class flips will require you to yield some control—always keep this truth in mind. We'll explore it more in the next section.

Mindset Challenge 3: Your Own Need for Control

The traditional educational setting has put teachers at the front of the classroom for too long. Relinquishing some control is a challenge for many educators. Many teachers believe that a considerable distance should exist between them and their students to gain respect and recognition as the authority in the classroom. However, in today's world, the teacher is expected to be a facilitator of learning rather than an ultimate authority.

How can you face your own resistance?

- **Let go!** In the words of Jane King (1993), teachers should stop being the "sage on the stage" and become the "guide on the side." Students will feel empowered in their own learning and achieve their full potential if they have autonomy, with teacher support. Avoid trying to control every single thing that happens in your classroom. Allow your lessons to flow organically. If you let go, you can help guide students in making their own learning decisions. You can let them choose and value different learning methods. When flipping, you build a learning culture that transforms students' and teachers' roles (Buitrago, 2017). Your students will likely be *more* cooperative and involved when you have *less* control over the class.

Mindset Challenge 4: Underestimating Students' Capabilities

Some teachers still view students as empty containers waiting for teachers to fill them with knowledge. This view of students is an obstacle in today's world and especially in flipped instruction. We have met teachers who believe their students cannot perform higher-order thinking tasks by themselves. Other teachers still consider students incapable of making their own learning decisions, regardless of their age. We've even seen teachers who make all the decisions for their students. If we do everything for students, how do we expect to have autonomous learners? What kind of message are we sending them?

How can you start changing your perception of students?

- **Give your students some credit.** Even at a young age, students can surprise you if you trust them. As Rita Pierson puts it in her TED talk (YEAR), every kid needs a champion. "Children just need an adult who trusts them and their capabilities and who believes they can excel." If as teachers we are the first ones who tell our students they can't do something, or that they need us to succeed, then how can we expect them to achieve their full potential autonomously? Similarly, when parents do homework for their young children; they are sending a very clear "you can't do it" message to them, which transforms capable kids into dependent, needy, and unsure individuals. Don't create this kind of dependency in your students.

- **We should trust our students, challenge them, and offer them the chance to make mistakes and to learn from them.** So while planning your in-class flip, don't be afraid to include some complex, higher-order thinking tasks, provide opportunities for students to assess each other and themselves, and encourage students to own their learning process by allowing them to make decisions. Show them that you trust their ability to excel.

Mindset Challenge 5: A Lack of Problem-Solving Skills

Do you panic when facing difficulties in the classroom? Do you feel the need to have control over every single detail so that issues don't emerge? Many hurdles can present themselves when you're planning your in-class flip. But running away from these hurdles won't help you develop and excel as a professional educator. Let's discuss a couple of points that can be lifesavers when any inconveniences emerge.

How can you prepare for unexpected teaching situations?

Be willing to make on-the-spot decisions by anticipating possible problems. One of the best ways to feel confident in taking action when a difficulty arises is to prepare for it. Take lifeguarding as an example. The reason why so much time and money is invested in training lifeguards is that if they train long enough with many scenarios, they are more likely to know what to do when a situation emerges. Teaching in an in-class flip should be viewed in the same way. We need to foresee possible hurdles and think of ways to solve them on the spot. We, the authors, experienced many hurdles as we implemented our flips in the past; now you can benefit from our mistakes.

- **Miscalculation:** Say you plan a group activity for your class, but some of your students don't come; consequently, the number of students per group is no longer right.

  Solution: Renumber students to create new groups or group students in a different way (according to their zodiac sign or by color of clothing). For instance, if you have twenty students and you had planned to form five groups of four students, but only eighteen came to class, make six groups of three students and move on.

- **Difficult Material:** The content provided in class is harder for students to grasp than you expected, and it's taking them longer to understand the information.

  Solution: If you are doing station work, remove one station. (Don't worry! You can always do that activity at another time.) Also, when planning the stations, anticipate this possibility and plan some lower-order thinking tasks that you can easily remove or replace. Remember that you can do station work over more than one day. If, on the other hand, you are doing a solo, duo, or group flip, let students take the time they need. Don't rush the lesson to get to the practice activities because you are on a schedule. Understanding content is key to mastering the topic, so be flexible and make adjustments.

- **Not Enough Time:** You designed too many stations and students seem anxious about not having the ability or the time to finish all of them.

  Solution: Change the schedule! Nobody said you have to do your entire in-class flip in only one class session. A successful and complete in-class flip may take two class sessions, and that is okay. Remember, your students will be learning at a deeper level, so taking a bit more time to visit all the stations will do them more benefit than harm.

- **Too Much Time:** You designed a station you thought would be harder for students, and it turned out to be simple. Suddenly you're faced with a lot of fast finishers.

  Solution: Have students switch if there are two of these stations. Alternately, have an independent station for fast finishers where students can go to play a game, solve a problem, write a questionnaire, etc.

What you know about your class and your students will dictate your practices. Adopt what Carol Dweck called "the growth mindset." It will definitely be a game changer for you. If you are reading this book, and you have gotten this far, it means you already have this mindset (or are working towards it) and are ready to create a remarkable change in your classroom.

Challenges in Planning

The second type of obstacles we have identified involve planning. Doing an in-class flip for the first couple of times may be challenging, because of the level of detail and planning. Luckily, we have gone through the process many times. In this following section, we will share our insights so you can avoid the same mistakes and difficulties.

Planning Challenge 1: Time

Lesson planning is a time-consuming activity. And planning for an in-class flip may pose extra challenges, because many of the activities are simultaneous. You need to visualize the flip and draw your "in-class flip blueprint." Prepare your resources, make copies, draw or print your station signs, record your instructional videos, create or curate content, etc. Planning time should become similar to the time you spend planning a traditional class, especially when you have more experience.

To read about in-class flips done by the authors, scan the QR codes below.

Martha's in-class flip   Carolina's in-class flip
bit.ly/3jeaVDY   **bit.ly/3fGlY6K**

How can I optimize my planning time in the long run?

- **Think ahead.** When planning your syllabus at the beginning of the year, try to identify the topics you may want to cover in an in-class flip. That way, you can start thinking in advance about the content and practice materials you will have to prepare. You may find that you already have material from previous courses that you can convert into an in-class flip.

- **Prepare long-lasting materials, and reuse them.** The first time you launch a new strategy, planning will be more time consuming. For example, the first time you set up any of the station-rotation configurations, it is going to take extra time and effort. So, prepare long-lasting materials, and reuse them. Laminate and reuse board games, card games, cutouts, copies, etc. Create and laminate general station signs so you can simply add masking tape with the name of the activity you will do that day. Be mindful of the future, and anytime you can, create materials that can be reused.

- **Organize material for immediate use and future reference.** Besides making long-lasting materials, it is crucial to organize them for future access. If you develop digital materials, make sure to save them in an easily retrievable file you can find the next time you teach that same class. Nothing is more frustrating than taking the time to create something awesome and then not finding it because you forgot where you saved it. If you make physical material, you can label it and have a specific container or drawer in which to store it safely. You could also do what Jon Bergmann did in his labs: "I would have plastic tubs with everything I needed to do a given activity. And then when I came back to it the next year or the next semester, all I had to do was grab that tub."

Planning Challenge 2: Space Organization

For an in-class flip to work well, some flexibility in the space is needed. Students need to be able to physically navigate the areas where the content is presented, so having a flexible space is ideal. Unfortunately, some classrooms have static desks and limited spaces. Flexibility then depends on your creativity to find a way to optimize your use of the space. Regardless of your spatial limitations, in-class flipping is still possible.

How can I organize my space for an in-class flip?

Be resourceful and work with what you have. We managed to pull off a great in-class flip session in an auditorium with immovable seating. You can do it too! Some ideas for optimizing the space you have include:

- **The floor:** You can ask students to sit on the floor for specific activities that require a large, flat surface—like making a poster.

- **Chairs:** If you do not have tables, you can use chairs as tables.

- **Walls:** Walls can become stations. Ask students to stand up and rotate along the walls while completing different tasks.

- **Outdoors:** Go outside if you need more space and weather permits.

Don't feel discouraged if adapting your space doesn't seem easy. Students won't mind where and how their learning is taking place, as long as it is meaningful to them. They will be willing to be flexible with the resources you have as long as you show your willingness to make the best of it.

Planning Challenge 3: Student Organization

Just as planning space can be a hassle, organizing students for an in-class flip can also be a challenge. Thinking about the many aspects involved can be a daunting task, however, doing so will optimize instruction.

What should I keep in mind to organize my students?

Be flexible when deciding on the grouping criteria for your in-class flip. Compose a list of grouping strategies that include (but are not exclusive to):

- **Skill Level:** Group students according to their skill level so that you have more and less proficient students working together in a group. The in-class flip layout can allow for in-class tutoring to happen if you use this kind of grouping.

- **Interests:** Sometimes you can group students by their different interests in life. Students will show preferences for some topics over others, and you can use that to your advantage. Have musicians, sports fans, fashion geeks, computer geeks, gamers, environmentalists, animalists, vegans, Instagrammers, etc., work together in class.

- **Students' Learning Preference:** Allow students to work according to their learning preferences. Have kinesthetic, visual, and auditory learners group together and work on tasks planned for their learning preference in particular.

- **Random Grouping:** You can also group your students with no pedagogical interest in particular but simply to mingle them. For instance, you can give students numbers one through five (repeating) and have them group according to the number they got. But, if you are feeling more creative, you can use the techniques we use in our classes, which we explain below.

- **Poker Cards:** Count the number of students you have in class and make groups using poker cards before the class session begins. Count out from the deck the same number of poker cards as students, organized in twos or threes or fours **(i.e., fifteen students in your class correspond to: 3 aces + 3 jacks + 3 kings + 3 tens + 3 queens = 15 cards)**. Then, shuffle the cards and give one card per student. Afterwards, call out the card names and have students group with the people who have the same card.

- **Small Objects:** Give secret, small objects to students at the beginning of the class. You can give students assorted candy, colored stones, lollipop sticks, colored rods, colored pencils, stickers, toys, buttons, etc., at the beginning of the class and then use those to group them. You can say something like, "Green stones, you are a group."

Planning Challenge 4: Giving Clear Instructions

One of the biggest obstacles to staging a successful in-class flip is a lack of clear instructions. For example, when working in stations, clear instructions are crucial to avoid confusion and delays, since students start working at different points of the lesson. Poor instructions can mess up your entire class. Additionally, don't ignore

Figure 11.1. Grouping with playing cards.

students' different approaches to learning when planning instructions. Some learners may miss the point of what you want them to do.

How can I give clear instructions?

Make instructions visible. Giving flipped instructions might be challenging for some teachers, especially now that you're not giving the instructions verbally, yourself, but are depending on written, audio, or video instructions you've created or curated.

If your in-class flip is done in stations, we encourage you to create small posters and stick them to the wall or on the table in front of every station, so that when students are working, they can refer to the instructions at any moment. You can see how Martha posted instructions in one of her flips in Figure 11.2.

On the other hand, if your in-class flip is organized using in-situ work, you can make instructions available to students in many ways: post them on your classroom tables, or provide digital instructions through a video, Google doc, audio files, slides, a Wiki, etc.

Preparing clear instructions can be time consuming, but it is time worth spending, since your students will focus on activities only if they clearly understand the expectations. Some teachers might find the number of variables for planning an in-class flip intimidating; however, at least now you know what those variables are. Advance preparation really is key to a successful in-class flip.

EXAMPLES OF AN IN-CLASS FLIP
If you are curious of what an in-class flip looks like, check out these two examples

1. Check out a blog post about an in-class flip with a pronunciation lesson.

2. Check out a blog post with an in-class flip plan about teaching types of sentences.

Pronunciation post | **Sentences post**

Figure 11.2. Martha's station rotation instructions on flipped learning in a professional development workshop.

WHAT IS IN-CLASS FLIP?
Part 1 – Using stations

1. Scan the QR code

2. Watch the video with your group.

3. Answer the questions in the padlet.

VIDEO

Padlet: https://goo.gl/5RYhzr

REFLECTIVE PAUSE

Which of the challenges in this chapter scare you the most? Do you think the solutions proposed would help? Can you think of other possible solutions?

CHAPTER 12

Technology Tools That Support the In-Class Flip

This chapter addresses several ISTE Standards:

2.1. Learner
Educators continually improve their practice by learning from and with others and exploring proven and promising practices that leverage technology to improve student learning. Educators:

a. Set professional learning goals to explore and apply pedagogical approaches made possible by technology and reflect on their effectiveness.

2.2. Leader
Educators seek out opportunities for leadership to support student empowerment and success and to improve teaching and learning. Educators:

b. Advocate for equitable access to educational technology, digital content, and learning opportunities to meet the diverse needs of all students.

2.3. Citizen
Educators inspire students to positively contribute to and responsibly participate in the digital world. Educators:

> *b. Establish a learning culture that promotes curiosity and critical examination of online resources and fosters digital literacy and media fluency.*
>
> ## 2.5. Designer
> Educators design authentic, learner-driven activities and environments that recognize and accommodate learner variability. Educators:
>
> *b. Design authentic learning activities that align with content area standards and use digital tools and resources to maximize active, deep learning.*
>
> ## 2.6. Facilitator
> Educators facilitate learning with technology to support student achievement of the ISTE Standards for Students. Educators:
>
> *b. Manage the use of technology and student learning strategies in digital platforms, virtual environments, hands-on makerspaces, or in the field.*

REFLECTIVE PAUSE

Before you start this chapter, think about the technology you already use in your classroom and how you could integrate it into your in-class flips.

TECHNOLOGY CHANGES EVERY DAY. Today's innovative tool is tomorrow's most commonly-used app. Thus, it can be difficult to talk about technologies in a world where a new tool emerges by the minute. We will share the tech tools that have facilitated our own in-class flip implementations. You will have to decide which tools to use yourself. Some of these tools are best used for planning your in-class flip, and others are best for executing it in the classroom.

Timing Students' Work

Digital tools are helpful for tracking time. For example, when doing a sequenced station rotation, timing is crucial. Interrupting highly engaged students at every station is difficult and time consuming. By using one of the online timers suggested in Table 12.1, you can ease the situation and still have control of the time spent at each station. Any timer (on your smartphone or tablet, a kitchen timer, a chronometer) will do the job as well. Use tools you feel most comfortable with.

TABLE 12.1 Digital Timers

TOOL		DESCRIPTION
Egg Timer e.ggtimer.com		An utterly simple interface that displays a screen-size timer with a noisy beep when time is up.
Online Timer online-stopwatch.com/ countdown-timer		This site offers a wider variety of clock designs (sand clock, chess clock, etc.). The alternative timer layouts are appealing to students. Watch the volume as the "time's up" noise can be quite loud for certain options.

TABLE 12.2 Tools for Video and Screencast

	TOOL		DESCRIPTION
CREATING SCREENCASTS	**Slides + screencast-o-matic** screencast-o-matic.com **View a sample screencast** bit.ly/3eDZphY		By far, the easiest tool we have found to create nice and straightforward videos. It is easy to use, offers 15 minutes of recordings, and has a variety of options for video storage (Screencast-o-matic dashboard, YouTube and MP4).
CREATING VIDEOS	**Du Recorder** du-recorder.com **Watch a video demonstration** bit.ly/2B8lWWg **View a sample of a video recorded with Du Recorder** (edited using We video) bit.ly/2OCw3W		When Martha's laptop broke down, she found the Du Recorder app, which allowed her to replace the laptop with her phone. With this app, you can record yourself on video or screencast slides on your phone. The quality and sound is great. Plus, you have the tool right inside your pocket, so you can make a video virtually anywhere. The app is free and unlimited in the video extension. Only as much as your phone memory allows.

Creating Videos

You might decide to share the content of your lesson via video. As usual, the simpler the tool, the better. Bergmann and Sams (2012) wonder, "Do you want your video perfect, or do you want it by Tuesday?" Table 12.2 offers a variety of tools for creating videos and screencasts and Table 12.3 shares some of our favorite tools for designing content. When students access content on their own, we want to guarantee they are focused and engaged. We want to help students get the most out of the materials they consume. Adding interactivity to videos facilitates this process. Over time, it also helps students learn how to focus on and engage with all videos, not just those that offer the above features.

TABLE 12.3 **Tools for Designing Content**

	TOOL		DESCRIPTION
MAKING DESIGNS	**Canva** canva.com		There are many sites for creating visuals. Yet, the one we have used the most because of its great designs, user-friendliness and options is Canva. You can create nice-looking posters to show your students any topic. Some other options you can create include graphic organizers, slides, CVs, worksheets, infographics, and shareable images to social media.
DESIGNING FLIPPED CONTENT	**Genial.ly** genial.ly **Example of an in-class flip sequenced configuration** bit.ly/3sbOvcR		One of our go-to tools for designing flipped content because of its myriad of options and interactivity. Ideal for online, face-to-face, and hybrid settings, use it to design virtual stations, in-situ content, games, quizzes, lesson plans, presentations, infographics, comics, and more.

TABLE 12.4 Tools for Video-Watching Accountability

TOOL		DESCRIPTION
Playposit learn.playposit.com/learn		Playposit is a complete platform to add interactivity to your videos and to guarantee students' deeper learning. It offers different types of questions (free response, multiple choice, and reflective pause are available in the free version). It also has a monitoring tool that allows teachers to track students' work.
Edpuzzle edpuzzle.com		Edpuzzle offers a mobile app that facilitates students' work with videos. It has options for adding voice notes and files to the video activities. You can create ten lessons for free with all the features.

Video-Watching Accountability

Flipped learning has grown exponentially. More and more websites that facilitate flipping emerge every day. An important part of many flipped learning settings is the need to hold students accountable for content that they watch. Table 12.4 suggests two websites that are great for holding students accountable because of their ease of use.

Another great use of these websites is the personalization of curated content. Your busy schedule and discomfort with video making don't have to interfere with your desire to flip your classroom. You can find videos on sites like YouTube or Vimeo and personalize them. Using the above tools, you can add comments, reflections, and questions to these videos, modifying them to fit your students' needs.

Reading Accountability

You don't need videos to flip your class. Sometimes your students might get as much knowledge (or even more) from a text. But we need to think of ways to guarantee that students understand the text thoroughly. Sometimes students lack the strategies to read at a deep level and to maximize their learning. You can help them with a simple trick: manually annotating a reading. Table 12.5 shares a couple of web tools that offer this functionality.

TABLE 12.5

Tools for Reading Accountability

TOOL		DESCRIPTION
Actively Learn activelylearn.com		Actively Learn is a website that: • allows teachers to add interactivity to PDF files and other text formats. • adds comments, questions, highlights, vocabulary words, and more. • engages students with the content, guaranteeing deeper levels of thinking.
Insert Learning insertlearning.com		Insert Learning is a Chrome extension that allows teachers to enhance *any* website. The power of this tool is infinite. You can highlight and annotate the text. You can add questions, vocabulary, images, and even links to videos. You can exploit the content of any website you want to work with.
Perusall perusall.com		Perusall is a website that was developed by professor Eric Mazur of Harvard University. The platform can be integrated into most major learning management systems, and it is free. Perusall is a great option if you want to move away from video as a way to present your content to students. Perusall is a social learning platform where teachers can • upload articles, PDFs, and even books for students to access. • turn reading assignments into engaging, collective activities. • highlight, comment, and discuss readings in real time online.

Planning Your In-Situ Lessons

Even though technology isn't *required* to plan your in-class flip lessons, the following tools can help you structure autonomous lessons for your students to tackle at their own pace.

TABLE 12.6

Tools for In-Situ Lessons

TOOL		DESCRIPTION
Google Suite google.com		For quality HyperDocs, all the tools in the Google Suite will come in handy. They can help you integrate the different levels of Bloom's taxonomy. Consider linking to other tools discussed in this chapter.
Go Formative goformative.com		Go Formative: • generates entire lessons with their free tools. • uses ready-made lessons or a document of your own. • adds questions to make lessons interactive. • helps students work at their own pace without getting lost.
Padlet padlet.com		Padlet is a free digital wall that displays all your students' responses at once. Responses can be given in different ways. Students can add gifs, videos, or draw or write their responses. It is useful for feedback and students' questions.
Flipgrid bit.ly/3jejwGW		Flipgrid is a digital wall on video. Students can respond to any of your questions via video. They can use an avatar if they don't feel particularly comfortable showing their face. With this tool, you can give feedback via email directly from the site, and students can comment on each other's videos. You can also easily integrate it into your online lessons.

With these tools, you can build automated accountability mechanisms. You can insert digital mastery checks at different stages of a lesson and check them later. With these tools in place, you can focus your attention on students' needs during the lesson.

Immediate Response Systems

A way to check if students understand and remember what they saw in a video is to create a station with gamified quizzes. Immediate response systems are online tools that allow teachers to prepare questions in advance. Students respond using their smartphones, tablets, or computers. Table 12.7 shares several engaging tools that allow students to revise their responses and check against correct answers (on their own or with the teacher). Their gamified nature offers excitement and a little bit of healthy pressure, engaging students.

TABLE 12.7
Immediate Response Systems

TOOL	DESCRIPTION
Kahoot! kahoot.com	Kahoot! is a great immediate response system, since it offers multiple quizzing options. It has quizzes (individual and team), polls, and jumble games. You can also send quizzes as homework.
Socrative socrative.com	Socrative offers the option to create quizzes (individual and team), space races, and exit tickets. You can choose from an array of options, including open-ended questions.
Plickers get.plickers.com	Plickers is a brilliant and low-tech immediate response system tool. With plickers you just print a set of QR codes representing answers. Students use them to show their answers instead of using electronic devices. You just need one phone (your own) to scan students' QR codes, and a presentation station in your classroom to show the questions.

Students find these tools engaging and fascinating. If you have trouble creating a station to check students' understanding of video, these tools can offer you and your students great fun. Using them helps learners internalize concepts.

Podcasting

Another great way of providing authentic content for your students is through podcasts. There are free podcasts available in all fields of knowledge and in all languages, making it a convenient resource. Also, many podcasting services allow the user to create their own channels and upload episodes they create. This generates opportunities for teacher and students to create their own episodes and make them available to the public, if desired.

You can also simply record yourself giving oral instructions for students to access on their own.

TABLE 12.8

Podcasting and Audio Recording Tools

TOOL	DESCRIPTION
Your own content	You can create your own recordings using free software, like Audacity, or with any recording app in your smartphone. You can make your own recordings as a way to give oral instructions for an activity in a station. For instance, you can make a "Mission Impossible" self-destructing message. Having the teacher's voice on a recording creates a certain mystery that spices stations up.
Spreaker spreaker.com	This tool is incredibly versatile since it has a multiplicity of topics from education to quantum physics. It also offers the chance for teachers to create their own channels for their classes. You can have the "podcast creating station" in one of your in-class flips, or assign an audio to listen to.

Games and Simulations

For students, games are a favorite. Many websites offer games to practice content or to create your own for learning purposes. We have also seen interesting simulations to help students to grasp concepts. It is just a matter of searching for something that can be adapted to your context.

Online games are a great way to engage students. If you have computers or tablets in your classroom, don't hesitate to prepare a station containing one of these games.

TABLE 12.9 Games and Simulations

TOOL		DESCRIPTION
Gamify Your Classroom bit.ly/3taPqLz		This site provides a list of game-based websites you can use to both create games and include pre-made games in your teaching. You will find a great variety to choose from!
Phet Interactive Simulations bit.ly/30kXhGL		In this site from The University of Colorado, Boulder, you can find science simulations for physics, biology, and chemistry. They are organized by grade level and topic.

REFLECTIVE PAUSE

Did you learn any new technology you could integrate into your in-class flips?

Your favorite tool:	Add description here:

THE IN-CLASS FLIP AROUND THE WORLD

"What students need is a teacher on demand. Sir Ken Robinson asked, 'How do you teach kids differently?' And to answer that question I can think of a metaphor. You know, back in 1928 we had black and white TV, then in 1950 or 60 we added color to it, but it was really not that different than the TV box of before. Then came Sky TV and Digital TV, and they were also pretty much the same. However, Netflix changed the paradigm,, because now you can choose how you want your show and when you want it, and we need to give our students that kind of choice." —Heath Chittenden, Principal, Ashhurst School, Ashhurst, New Zealand

CHAPTER 13

Rewiring Your Teaching Approach

> **This chapter addresses several ISTE Standards:**
>
> **2.1. Learner**
>
> Educators continually improve their practice by learning from and with others and exploring proven and promising practices that leverage technology to improve student learning. Educators:
>
> c. *Stay current with research that supports improved student learning outcomes, including findings from the learning sciences.*
>
> **2.2. Leader**
>
> Educators seek out opportunities for leadership to support student empowerment and success and to improve teaching and learning. Educators:
>
> c. *Model for colleagues the identification, exploration, evaluation, curation, and adoption of new digital resources and tools for learning.*
>
> **2.3. Citizen**
>
> Educators inspire students to positively contribute to and responsibly participate in the digital world. Educators:

a. *Create experiences for learners to make positive, socially responsible contributions and exhibit empathetic behavior online that build relationships and community.*

2.4. Collaborator

Educators dedicate time to collaborate with both colleagues and students to improve practice, discover and share resources and ideas, and solve problems. Educators:

a. *Dedicate planning time to collaborate with colleagues to create authentic learning experiences that leverage technology.*

b. *Collaborate and co-learn with students to discover and use new digital resources and diagnose and troubleshoot technology issues.*

c. *Use collaborative tools to expand students' authentic, real-world learning experiences by engaging virtually with experts, teams, and students, locally and globally.*

2.5. Designer

Educators design authentic, learner-driven activities and environments that recognize and accommodate learner variability. Educators:

a. *Use technology to create, adapt, and personalize learning experiences that foster independent learning and accommodate learner differences and needs*

b. *Design authentic learning activities that align with content area standards and use digital tools and resources to maximize active, deep learning.*

c. *Explore and apply instructional design principles to create innovative digital learning environments that engage and support learning.*

2.6. Facilitator

Educators facilitate learning with technology to support student achievement of the ISTE Standards for Students. Educators:

b. *Manage the use of technology and student learning strategies in digital platforms, virtual environments, hands-on makerspaces, or in the field.*

2.7. Analyst

Educators understand and use data to drive their instruction and support students in achieving their learning goals. Educators:

a. *Provide alternative ways for students to demonstrate competency and reflect on their learning using technology.*

THE IN-CLASS FLIP CAN ADAPT TO ANY PEDAGOGICAL APPROACH to make learning more student-centered. Whether your current teaching includes problem-based learning, gamification, mastery-based learning, or any other teaching approach, in-class flipping is a suitable option. Many teachers have already merged flipped learning with these different learning models successfully. We have gone a step further with the in-class flip.

Integrating Content and Language through the In-Class Flip

Content and language integrated learning (CLIL) is a dual-focused educational approach in which an additional language is used for the learning and teaching of both content and language, as defined by Do Coyle, Phillip Hood, and David Marsh (2010). This method is mostly used in European and Latin American countries. In the United States and Canada, the most common approaches to integrating language and content classes are SIOP (Sheltered Instruction Observation Protocol) and CBI (Content-Based Instruction). Even though these models are different in their planning and lesson delivery processes, they coincide in their mission to support English Language Learners' (or any other language learners') learning processes around the world.

Through CLIL, SIOP, and CBI, you can craft inclusive practices in your classrooms. Do you teach math, science, social studies, art? Do you have ELLs in your classroom, but you feel that teaching them English is not your responsibility? Inclusion is a *must* in today's world. Teaching content classes without accommodations for ELLs means leaving children behind. CLIL, SIOP, and CBI are a way to differentiate instruction for the ELLs in your class. In this section, we'll discuss how we have used them in our context (Colombia), so that you can get an idea of how these approaches, especially CLIL, might work. You may want to study them in depth to make them work for your own context.

Even though CLIL was born in Europe, many Latin American countries currently use it successfully. CLIL solved the educational challenges that arose from a need for mobility from country to country in Europe. CLIL promotes the Framework for 21st-Century Skills, and the idea that we need to educate students to be better citizens for the future. CLIL operates under the 4 Cs: Content, Communication, Cognition, and Culture:

- **Content:** the information you want your students to learn. It is what any teacher thinks about during lesson planning. What am I going to teach to my learners today? Is it the photosynthesis process? Is it the concept of fractions? Is it the art movements of the twentieth century in Europe? Is it the rules of a basketball match?

- **Communication:** refers to language. What different types of language will my ELL students need to perform the tasks I have planned for them in class? CLIL proponents suggest considering three types of language:

  1. Language of learning (content-specific vocabulary and structures needed to explain concepts and perform tasks)

  2. Language for learning (expressions and vocabulary necessary to communicate in a classroom situation, such as language for debates)

  3. Language through learning (the language that teachers can't plan for and that emerges throughout the lesson)

- **Cognition:** refers to the mental processing students will have to do with the information they receive. In this stage, the teacher can use Bloom's taxonomy to think of different cognitive tasks where she will encourage students to learn the content more deeply. Cognition also refers to the critical-thinking skills necessary for a student to succeed in today's classroom and world.

- **Culture:** refers to the level of connection between the content and students' real lives (impact on their surroundings, interaction with others and society). Through this lens we see how relevant our teaching and our class are to our students' lives.

Even though CLIL is not strictly a language-teaching method, most language educators know about it. But CLIL can serve well in *any* class to differentiate instruction and offer enriching experiences to ELLs. Below are links to a lesson plan format and a layout we created for in-class flipping a CLIL class. Feel free to make a copy of the formats and adapt them to your own learners.

CLIL lesson plan format
bit.ly/2MDmcgr

CLIL in-class flip layout format
bit.ly/2vFUbP7

How Can I Use CLIL in an In-Class Flip?

Specifying the communication aspect in your lesson plans can go a long way for students. Content teachers regularly think of making content they teach intentional. Also, most teachers use strategies for ensuring understanding, and thus cognition.

The cultural aspect is also well thought out. Yet, content teachers often don't think of the specific language (vocabulary, structures) students need to use in their classes. Following are a few tips on how you can integrate language in an in-class flip.

Create Anchor Charts with the Necessary Language
Anchor charts are visually appealing posters you can:

- design to ensure certain elements of your class are highly visible.

- preplan and create for the two types of languages (language of learning and language for learning) that students should have handy throughout the lesson.

- make via digital or manual means.

Prepare a Language Stop When Working with Stations
Remember: with CLIL we aim at differentiating instruction for your ELLs, so by having a "necessary language" station with expressions, vocabulary lists, and bilingual or multilingual posters or images, you can offer a great level of support to the ELLs in your class, and lso to any underachieving students who might benefit from some extra help.

Designate an "Emerging Language" Wall
Students' language questions will come up as they work with the content and complete cognitive tasks. Since you might not be a language expert, you can collect students' questions and address them during the following class with the help of the language instructor at your school. After doing this exercise several times, you will be able to predict the type of language with which your students struggle. As a result, you will be able to customize your anchor charts according to your students' needs.

Assign a Language Peer Mentor to Your ELLs
Teaching is one of the best ways to learn, so consider creating a peer-instruction scheme. Peer instruction is an effective strategy for educators. Your student mentors can be those students who excel at language-pattern recognition. They don't have to be language teachers; they could assist both ELLs and struggling learners in expressing ideas better.

Adapt Materials with Your ELLs in Mind
When you prepare content input, keep in mind your ELLs—add in a few questions to spark higher-order thinking, clarify challenging vocabulary, and point out important information you don't want them to miss because of language barriers. Add in a box or slide with key vocabulary. Keep them on your radar as you plan. As you can see, none of these tips demand that you become a linguist. However, making small additions like these to your lesson plans will make a substantial difference in your ELL students' learning.

REFLECTIVE PAUSE

Had you considered your ELLs in your planning? How did you integrate them into your lessons before? How do you plan to integrate them into your lessons now?

Project Based Learning

Dan Jones, a flipped project-based learning expert, defines project-based learning (PBL) as "the act of using a project as a learning tool for students to gain understanding as well as express their mastery of the curriculum" (2018, p. 2). In his view, when we pair the PBL teaching approach with flipped learning, PBL happens in the right way. According to Jones, flipped learning provides the time to do PBL consistently and in an integrated way by applying Bloom's taxonomy. Students are mainly focused on analyzing and creating. Through the product they create, students show application of their knowledge. Then, they evaluate the connection between the information they are using and the content learned before.

Jones asserts that through project-based learning, students can "demonstrate their learning in a way that is tangible and experiential" (Jones, 2018, p. 9). In PBL, students have choices in how to show their learning, and PBL stretches their understanding of the content. Jones proposes a five-elements structure to PBL:

1. Essential why and how questions that guide the process

2. Content within units of study

3. Student research as part of the learning

4. The creation of a product

5. The inclusion of the community

You can plan PBL lessons in different ways. We will provide examples of how you can do an in-class flip within Jones's structure. We also encourage you to adapt the examples to your own approach to project-based learning.

In his lesson planning structure, Jones proposes six steps:

1. Pre-Unit: Students research the essential questions provided for the project on their own.

2. Design Lab: This timed set of activities leads to exploration of the students' previous knowledge of the topic as well as collaborative peer learning. It consists of eleven short activities carried out in one or more lessons with a variety of individual, pair, and group work. At the end of the design lab process, students have constructed their idea of the project they wish to work on. For an in-depth description of this process, we recommend Jones's book *Flipped 3.0 Project Based Learning: An Insanely Simple Guide*.

3. Flipped Content: After the design lab, students access flipped content from home and come prepared to discuss what they have learned the next day. They discuss using what Jones has called "Turn 'n' Talk" cards, which contain guiding questions.

4. Labs and Activities: Students are then asked to do a number of labs or activities. Content-appropriate labs can be found in ready-made resources, or they can be created by each teacher, as in Jones's case, to fit specific needs.

5. Project Application Work: The application stage involves direct teacher support with applying and understanding the content.

6. Assessment: In the final step, students are assessed and made accountable for their learning.

The In-Class Flip and PBL

Your main focus should be on how students are supported in their understanding of the content, so they may apply it and create a project that reflects that understanding. When thinking about doing an in-class flip using PBL, the main elements to consider are the flipped content, the activities or labs, and project support.

Following are some tips on planning an in-class flip using PBL:

- Connect activities to essential questions. As you plan activities or labs, make sure they align with the content and with the questions students are trying to answer via the project. Focus activities on Bloom's higher-order thinking skills.

- Plan a content discussion station or activity. Whether you want to use question cards or encourage the discussion in another way (through a game, interview, etc.), find a way to get students talking. Provide opportunities for students to socialize while discussing their understanding of the content.

- Plan a "project idea" gallery activity. This activity could be a station within a linear lesson plan where you ask students to display their project ideas for their classmates. They can share their ideas through mini posters, sketchnotes, slides, audio recordings, videos, or posts on a learning management system. The purpose of this activity is for students to give each other feedback on their project ideas to improve the creation process. Students can give each other feedback through comments, voice notes, post-its, or stickers.

- Use a project feedback tracker. As you work with different students in providing support for their projects, track whom you have provided feedback to, as well as the main aspects of the projects that you need to follow up on. This is especially helpful for large classes.

To sum up, there are many ways in which PBL could be integrated into an in-class flip. A big upside is the variety and differentiation that you and your students will bring to the tasks that a project requires.

REFLECTIVE PAUSE

Have you integrated projects into your lessons? Which in-class flip configuration could you use? Can you think of other configurations?

Mastery Learning

Cara Johnson has described "flipped mastery" as "an instructional strategy in which students learn at a flexible pace" (2018, p. 1). The focus of this strategy is to address every learner's needs in the most personalized way possible. Using this model, the teacher guides individual students or groups of students to help them reach the learning goals that have been set for them. Students do not move on to a new objective until they have shown mastery of the current one.

According to Johnson (2018), there are five main benefits of this model:

1. Elimination of learning gaps
2. Flexible pacing
3. A value for mistakes
4. More academic success
5. Higher expectations for students (p. 2)

With this in mind, Johnson proposes a lesson cycle consisting of four main parts:

1. **Pre-Work:** Students access the new concepts and/or skills at home or in class.

2. **Practice and Learn:** These activities are focused on the new content. Students practice it and show their understanding of their learning.

3. **Mastery Check:** students show their understanding of the pre-work and practice and learn activities. If students fail to prove mastery, they complete more practice activities until they can show mastery of the topic at hand.

4. **Summative Assessment:** Students demonstrate their more global understanding of how all the objectives connect. If they are unsuccessful, they can do remediation activities before attempting the assessment again (p. 6).

The In-Class Flip and Flipped Mastery

Johnson (2018) has mentioned that the in-class flip is "a strategy that works perfectly for a Flipped Mastery Learning course" (p. 8), because it provides choice, varied pace, and differentiation, among other benefits. Pacing is the key element that will determine the configurations that best fit flipped mastery. If students are not given the flexibility to work at their own pace, then for some, demonstrating mastery of any type of content will be more difficult to achieve. All the in-class flip configurations can allow students to show mastery, as long as the way in which the teacher has planned them allows student flexibility.

In-situ work can ease "practice and learn" activities. Students can work with the flipped content and move through objectives at their own pace. Consider providing students with a lesson-mastery work plan to follow. In it, students would have the learning objectives, along with their corresponding "practice and learn" activities. With this plan, students can self-manage the process.

For station work, consider any of these ideas:

- **Half 'n' half:** For tutoring or feedback

- **Mixed:** For practice activities, including a teacher support station

- **Sequenced:** For scaffolded mastery checks

- **Looped:** With different flipped stations

Keep in mind the following tips for mastery learning in an in-class flip:

- **Provide a "lesson mastery" work plan.** Whether you use station or in-situ work, it is helpful for students to know where they can go next. The work plan could be a list of learning objectives and their associated activities organized sequentially.

- **Provide a teacher support station.** When you do an in-class flip to support the flipped mastery model, the teacher support station is necessary. Since students work at their own pace and rotate to the different activities, questions will always emerge. Having a teacher support station lets students know they can always find help when they need it.

Offer a variety of mastery checks—having a variety of mastery checks helps students face the challenge of completely mastering the material before moving on.

TEACHING SPOTLIGHT

In her high school biology class, Cara designed a mastery lesson where students had to demonstrate their understanding of the heart and the body's arteries and veins. She arranged her classroom in various stations and work spaces. Cara used a mixed configuration, which provided flexibility for tasks to happen at the same time. Some students worked on their mastery checks on laptops while others completed worksheets; some did drawings of veins and arteries; and others worked on dissecting hearts at designated tables. In the meantime, Cara monitored and provided feedback, unlocked the mastery checks when students were ready, and provided additional explanations when needed.

To see Cara in action, scan the QR code or visit **bit.ly/2OCELUC**.

"The in-class flip allowed for me to create a mastery learning environment. Students learn differently; therefore, they need the information at different points in their learning progressions. Allowing students to watch videos in class at their choosing provides the just-in-time instruction students need to continue to move forward in their understanding."—Cara Johnson, Allen Independent School District, Allen, Texas, U.S.A

Flipped mastery learning relies heavily on in-class flipping in offering students' choice and diverse pacing. Students benefit greatly from having different ways to access content and practice at different moments in the lesson. These two strategies combine seamlessly, creating the learning environment necessary for mastery to occur.

Gamifying Your In-Class Flip

One definition of *gamification* is "the process of adding games or game-like elements to something (such as a task) to encourage participation." For a long time, teachers have played games in the classroom to engage students and have them integrate their new knowledge with their background knowledge. These days, more and more, educators are using the systematic integration of game-like elements into regular activities to make them more appealing and engaging for the learner. In her latest book, *Hacking Digital Learning Strategies: 10 Ways to Launch EdTech Missions in Your Classroom* (2017), Shelly Sanchez Terrell puts forth another alternative: mission-minded learning. Shelly says that because missions are tied to meaningful purposes, "We should tie school lessons and activities to meaningful purposes that move beyond making good grades and passing tests" (p. 151). These models refresh our classes and integrate what students like and want to do.

Gamification

Have you ever been given a "frequent shopper card"? It's one of those cards issued by a store where they punch a hole or give you a sticker every time you make a new purchase, and after a certain number of purchases, you are rewarded in some way. Stores that choose to offer these cards are offering you a gamified experience. Surprised? Gamification is all around us! Let's look at it in depth.

When you think of gamification, you might think of badges, leader boards, or systems of reward, which are indeed simple forms of gamification. But today, gamification has gone far beyond these strategies. In 2014, Yu-Kai Chou proposed a framework for gamification called Octalysis. He put forth the existence of eight core drives for learning that can be extracted from the world of games, and he categorized these drives according to brain hemispheres and the tasks performed by each of them, and also by positive or negative affordances. The name Octalysis refers to the octagonal shape of the figure representing the framework. Yu-Kai Chou's Octalysis framework for gamification is shown in Figure 13.1. To hear the framework explained in detail, scan the QR code or visit **bit.ly/30I4bM6**.

As seen in Figure 13.1, there are some salient strategies in games that make them engaging—and that could improve the user experience in many fields, education included. Chou claims that "Everything we do is based on one of the eight core drives within Octalysis" (p. 3).

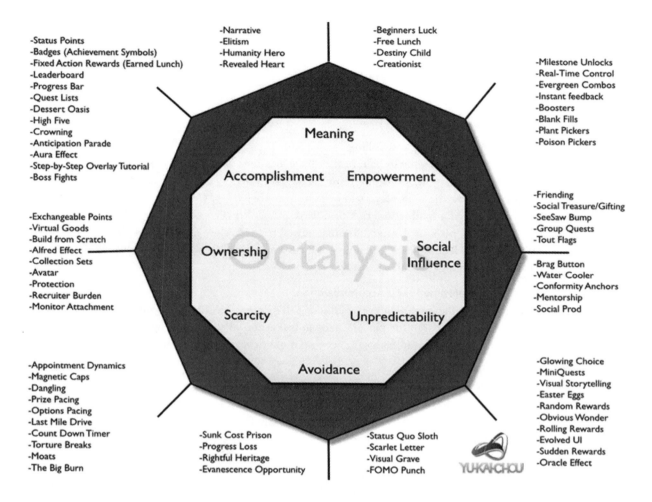

-Status Points
-Badges (Achievement Symbols)
-Fixed Action Rewards (Earned Lunch)
-Leaderboard
-Progress Bar
-Quest Lists
-Dessert Oasis
-High Five
-Crowning
-Anticipation Parade
-Aura Effect
-Step-by-Step Overlay Tutorial
-Boss Fights

-Narrative
-Elitism
-Humanity Hero
-Revealed Heart

-Beginners Luck
-Free Lunch
-Destiny Child
-Creationist

-Milestone Unlocks
-Real-Time Control
-Evergreen Combos
-Instant feedback
-Boosters
-Blank Fills
-Plant Pickers
-Poison Pickers

-Exchangeable Points
-Virtual Goods
-Build from Scratch
-Alfred Effect
-Collection Sets
-Avatar
-Protection
-Recruiter Burden
-Monitor Attachment

-Friending
-Social Treasure/Gifting
-SeeSaw Bump
-Group Quests
-Tout Flags

-Brag Button
-Water Cooler
-Conformity Anchors
-Mentorship
-Social Prod

-Appointment Dynamics
-Magnetic Caps
-Dangling
-Prize Pacing
-Options Pacing
-Last Mile Drive
-Count Down Timer
-Torture Breaks
-Moats
-The Big Burn

-Sunk Cost Prison
-Progress Loss
-Rightful Heritage
-Evanescence Opportunity

-Status Quo Sloth
-Scarlet Letter
-Visual Grave
-FOMO Punch

-Glowing Choice
-MiniQuests
-Visual Storytelling
-Easter Eggs
-Random Rewards
-Obvious Wonder
-Rolling Rewards
-Evolved UI
-Sudden Rewards
-Oracle Effect

Meaning

Accomplishment   Empowerment

Ownership   Social Influence

Scarcity   Unpredictability

Avoidance

YUKAICHOU

Figure 13.1. Yu-Kai Chou's Octalysis framework for gamification.
Reprinted from Actionable Gamification Beyond Points, Badges, and
Leaderboards (p. 1) by Y.K. Chou. Learn Pub. 2016.

Let's explore the core drives:

- Core Drive 1: Epic Meaning and Calling
- Core Drive 2: Development and Accomplishment
- Core Drive 3: Empowerment of Creativity and Feedback
- Core Drive 4: Ownership and Possession

- Core Drive 5: Social Influence and Relatedness
- Core Drive 6: Scarcity and Impatience
- Core Drive 7: Unpredictability and Curiosity
- Core Drive 8: Loss and Avoidance

Let's examine each core drive in detail.

Core Drive 1: Epic Meaning and Calling

This core drive allows people to believe they have a calling to accomplish a task or quest of great importance. For example, strategy games like *Age of Mythology* appeal to this core drive by allowing players to behave as noble heroes. Chou uses the example of Wikipedia to illustrate this core drive in real life. People who contribute to Wikipedia do it without the need for an external reward. They do it because by contributing, they feel they are protecting and disseminating knowledge; a worthwhile task with meaning bigger than themselves (p. 3).

Core Drive 2: Development and Accomplishment

Many kinds of gamification are developed using this core drive. Reward points, badges, and leader boards appeal to the player's need to feel accomplished. Moving from one level to the next, earning that badge, or scoring higher every time you play are strong motivators.

Core Drive 3: Empowerment of Creativity and Feedback

In Chou's words, "Empowerment of Creativity and Feedback is expressed when users are engaged in a creative process where they repeatedly figure things out and try different combinations" (p. 4). People feel engaged when they have the opportunity to create and when they receive feedback to improve the work they're doing. In our classrooms we must provide students with opportunities to create. When this happens organically, students' willingness to work and cooperate greatly increases.

Core Drive 4: Ownership and Possession

We work more enthusiastically if we own the project we are working on. This core drive moves learners to work towards the improvement of projects and processes they own. In Chou's words, "Ownership and Possession is where users are motivated because they feel like they own or control something" (p. 4).

Core Drive 5: Social Influence and Relatedness

This core drive refers to the social forces that drive our actions. These forces might provide positive motivation, but we can be provoked to action by negative feelings like jealousy and anger as well.

Core Drive 6: Scarcity and Impatience

This core drive appeals to our desire for what we can't or don't have. In Chou's words, "Scarcity and Impatience is the Core Drive of wanting something because it is extremely rare, exclusive, or immediately unattainable." Many games incorporated "appointment dynamics or torture breaks," (Chou, p. 5) which deprive the user of the game for a couple hours creating an urge in the user to go back to it again.

Core Drive 7: Unpredictability and Curiosity

Not knowing what is going to happen next, and yet wanting to, is the force behind this core drive. Chou asserts that "When something does not fall into your regular pattern recognition cycles, your brain kicks into high gear and pays attention to the unexpected" (p. 5).

Core Drive 8: Loss and Avoidance

According to Chou, this core drive "[is] the motivation to avoid something negative" (p. 6). Examples include missing the only opportunity to buy a certain product or to enjoy certain services. This core drive moves us to try to avoid losing out on opportunities.

These core drives are often considered when gamifying to strongly engage the user. Can you imagine ways that you could use the drives to enhance your classroom experiences? But before exploring how to use them with your in-class flip, let's take a look at another concept: Game-Based Learning.

Game-Based Learning

To make learning "irresistible," the Institute of Play in New York City developed what they called the Game-Like Learning Principles, which "bring together the principles of game design and learning design" using seven different core ideas. (Connected Learning Alliance, n.d.). The institute created Quest Schools based upon the idea that students learn better when they are playing, and they transformed the way these schools teach everything. Even though the Institute of Play shut down in 2019, their principles are still valid and their materials live within the Connected Learning Lab. The seven core ideas for game-like learning are:

- Everyone is a participant.

- Failure is framed as iteration.

- Learning feels like play.

- Learning happens by doing.

- Feedback is immediate and ongoing.

- Challenge is constant.

- Everything is interconnected.

Let's examine the principles further.

Everyone Is a Participant

In games, all players are included, and so it should be in class too. Nobody is left out. This principle implies the need for inclusion and differentiation. When you design a good game for your learners, you need to consider everyone and make sure every student will have a role within it.

Failure Is Reframed as Iteration

Learning should undergo a process of testing and iteration, and failure can be the opportunity to learn ways of doing things differently. As the famous quote by Thomas Alva Edison says: "I have not failed. I've just found 10,000 ways that won't work." As Carol Dweck mentions in her book Mindset, acknowledging that failure is not permanent, but just not being ready "yet" builds the growth mindset in our students. If we teach them that it is okay to fail and learn from that experience, every failure takes them a step closer towards success.

Learning Feels Like Play

Playing is engaging, user-centered, and it allows for decision making and creativity. Learning should not be any different. By creating a narrative in our lessons that will take students places and help them imagine a new world, we can engage them further in the learning process. So, instead of giving students a list of equations to solve, we can create a narrative around it by making students astronauts measuring distances between orbits and finding a good spot for landing. We can call it a mission and have students completely immersed in the equations in a fun way.

Learning Happens by Doing

Throughout this book, and all the flipped learning models, you have seen this principle. Learning should be active, and students should be central. Students learn by creating projects and solving problems, by deciding how to do things, and by getting their hands on the materials.

Feedback Is Immediate and Ongoing

In most games, you know how you are doing at all times. In a gamified lesson (and indeed all lessons), you should give students the rules of the game at the outset (assessment rubrics), so they know exactly how to succeed.

Challenge is Constant

Achieving the right level of challenge is not easy, but doing so, can keep students engaged and empowered to solve the puzzle. Games keep users engaged by providing the right level of challenge at every step. As users overcome harder obstacles, they level up. Also, challenges are designed with an increasing level of difficulty that keeps the user interested. In designing learning opportunities, the right amount of difficulty is also key. If we give our students a task that is too easy, the class becomes boring; and if we give them a task that is beyond their capabilities, it becomes too hard.

Everything Is Interconnected

Students can share what they do with other learning communities and find out connections among themselves and others. Online gaming has brought learners around the world together in the same screen. Online learning can also do the same by giving opportunities to students to connect with real people and their settings, and to field test what they are learning. For example, two teachers in different parts of the world teaching each other's language can bring the classes together via web conferencing tools to practice.

How Can I Use Gamification and Game-Based Learning in My In-Class Flip?

Even though these two concepts are not the same and cannot be used interchangeably, we can devise learning experiences that include both to enhance our students' interest and motivation. Games are enticing and effective for learners. Gamification and game-like learning help us to design lessons that students actually enjoy. Following are some ways in which you can integrate the core drives of gamification and the principles of game-like learning into your in-class flip planning.

Gamify Feedback

Make a feedback station and gamify it. Have students record their feedback before they leave the classroom, and penalize those who don't with something silly to do or by asking them to bring something to share next class.

Create Practice Games for Stations

Use the Institute of Play's Design Pack, downloadable from their website, to learn about game components and discover tips on how to create or "mod" your own games. You can create all sorts of board and card games to enhance the learning experience for your students.

Repurpose Your Own Home Games

We have repurposed Twister, UNO, Jenga, Parcheesi, poker, and other home games to meet the needs of our students. Just think about the rules of the original game, think about your students' needs and wants, and combine the two into a new version of your game.

Figure 13.2. Carolina's students playing "Sustainable Development Speaking Twister."

Transform a Station Rotation into a Quest

If you are planning a station rotation, call it a quest and have every step of the way become a mission. Shelley Sanchez Terrell (2017) talks about the power of mission-minded learning. She says, "We should tie school lessons and activities to meaningful purposes that go beyond making good grades and passing tests" (p. 151). If we create missions and quests, we are incorporating the "epic meaning" core drive of gamification. Students get a sense of purpose that taps into their imaginations and gives them an overall bigger reason to complete the stations.

Adding games to your lessons doesn't trivialize them. Games simply contribute to the overall generation of good feelings in your classroom. Games can engage your learners and make them more committed to the lesson at hand. Will you give games a try?

Uno –s endings game

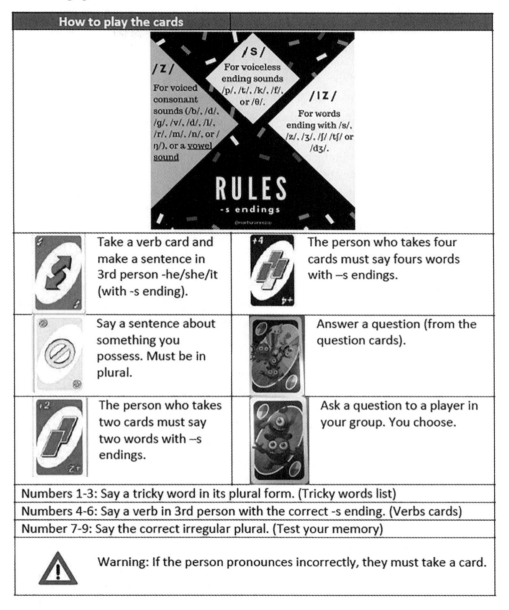

How to play the cards	
Take a verb card and make a sentence in 3rd person -he/she/it (with -s ending).	The person who takes four cards must say fours words with –s endings.
Say a sentence about something you possess. Must be in plural.	Answer a question (from the question cards).
The person who takes two cards must say two words with –s endings.	Ask a question to a player in your group. You choose.

Numbers 1-3: Say a tricky word in its plural form. (Tricky words list)

Numbers 4-6: Say a verb in 3rd person with the correct -s ending. (Verbs cards)

Number 7-9: Say the correct irregular plural. (Test your memory)

⚠ Warning: If the person pronounces incorrectly, they must take a card.

Figure 13.3. Martha's UNO game for pronunciation of -s endings.

Online Learning

In the words of Tony Bates, "Online learning is any form of learning conducted partly or wholly over the internet"(2016). In an online program, it is exciting to think that students can access materials and content anytime, anywhere. But, this ubiquitous access to information and the responsibility of learners to process all the content on their own pose critical challenges to the instructional designer.

In an online program, pedagogy has to drive instruction; technology cannot and should not be the driver. For that reason, instructional designers need to create programs that step beyond building online repositories. In an online environment, where students are alone at home and have limited access to the instructor for questions, clarity is key. Teachers need to design lessons that include learners' needs and interests. They also need to be intentional in the selection of materials and resources. Also, the scaffolding of activities so that learners may succeed on their own is pivotal.

When designing materials for the online setting, it is important to guarantee what Garrison, et al. (2000) called the three presences: teaching presence, cognitive presence, and social presence (p. 87). These concepts present the different needs students have when in an online environment. The instructional designer should include them when planning for more effective teaching. Let's examine the three presences.

Teaching Presence

This refers to the ability that online teachers have to craft effective learning experiences for all their learners through decision making in course design, the inclusion of materials, and the process of assessment and monitoring within the online space. Regardless of their readiness, interests, or levels of online learning experience, all students can succeed. Anderson and his colleagues define teaching presence as "the design, facilitation and direction of cognitive and social processes for realizing personally meaningful and educationally worthwhile learning outcomes" (p. 5). Just as in a physical classroom, the teacher is crucial for designing the best possible pathways for learners.

Cognitive Presence

This refers to students' cognitive engagement with concepts at a deeper level. In a study from 2003, Pawan et al. found that students normally feel more comfortable staying in the exploration mode of their learning while in an online environment and that it takes a direct intervention of the teacher in the form of comments, questions, and probing to move the process to higher stages of critical thinking and cognitive processing. Simply put, the teacher's intervention is necessary for students to reach the higher levels of processing seen in Bloom's taxonomy, and for the learning experience to flourish, students need to go higher and higher in their cognitive abilities.

Social Presence

This refers to the creation of social scenarios where students may share learning and explore content with other learners. As psychologist Lev Vygotsky indicated, learning is social and the construction of knowledge can only happen with the help of others (1978, p. 39). In online learning it is pivotal to have "spaces" where students may share, ask, and grow, not only as a learners, but also as people. Thus, opportunities to share personal information, build relationships, and speak one's mind about current events should also make part of the online classroom.

The teacher or instructional designer should consider the three presences to make the learning experience richer. Nowadays, most platforms offer technological tools that can ease the humanization of the online classroom, so teachers can craft meaningful learning experiences. However, online learning still tends to feel lonely for learners. So, the face of the teacher and synchronous interaction with peers can go a long way. Thus, the SOFLA® model, created by Helaine Marshall, comes in handy.

SOFLA®

SOFLA stands for the Synchronous Online Flipped Learning Approach, which "represented the wedding of two previously discrete modes of course delivery: Flipped Learning and synchronous online learning" (Marshall & Rodriguez-Buitrago, 2017, para. 6). In this model, there is room for an in-class flip component within the synchronous session.

Let us break a SOFLA lesson down for you. As in a regular flipped class, the teacher prepares and assigns content for students to work on individually. However, in an online course, students have to do more work independently than during class. Then, students work their way up the tiers of Bloom's taxonomy by doing tasks whose objectives aim at developing higher cognitive levels every time. As they read the materials from the textbook, watch the video lesson and take notes on it, and prepare their products, students are getting ready for the class. Then, there is a synchronous meeting via an academic platform (there are many available in the market now). The synchronous session observes a regular class structure.

- Warm-up activities

- Announcements by the teacher

- An activity to answer any questions that emerged while accessing the materials independently

- Practice activities (in the form of an in-class flip) in breakout rooms

- At class end everybody returns to the main room for debriefing.

Marshall and Kostka (2020) present a revised version of the model and suggestions for teachers. In SOFLA, the synchronous session is the culmination of a unit, and then you repeat the process with every unit in the syllabus.

How Can In-Class Flipping Enrich My Online Environment?

If you are an online educator wanting to spice up your lessons, then we want to contribute with our ideas! Following are some thoughts on how you can structure your stations and work with an in-class flip in an online environment.

Optimize Your Online Classroom by In-Class Flipping Using Breakout Rooms

Most online classrooms (Blackboard Collaborate, WIZiq, Adobe Connect, etc.) have a "breakout rooms" feature that allows you to split students into small groups within the online space. So why lecture when you can have students working actively to solve problems and collaborate? To create an in-class flip session using breakout rooms, you can follow the process below:

- Create different breakout rooms and name them (most platforms allow you to label breakout rooms differently).

- Create a path or a learning route (in online environments it is better to plan sequenced rotations since the teacher needs to manually move students from one breakout room to the next).

- Show a slide with the path on the whiteboard (even if students are in breakout rooms they can see the class whiteboard, so use it! Don't just have a blank page).

- Give clear instructions for students to follow while in each breakout room.

- Set a timer (in most platforms the timer will be a visible clock appearing on the screen and ringing at the end). This will signal that the time to move to the next station has arrived.

- Think carefully of the time students will take with the activity (and remember to have a Plan B, since technical issues might generate difficulties in your class session).

- Think of an outcome for students to complete while in every station. A shared product is desirable (wiki, collaborative document, Padlet wall) so that every student can see what the others have contributed and construct from there.

- By the end of the in-class flip activity, bring all students back to the main room and analyze the collaborative products together.

- Close your lesson with a whole-class activity that allows you to see whether students understand the information shared.

Humanize the Online Classroom with the In-Class Flip

Students in online programs (at least in the one where Carolina worked) commented on the loneliness they felt in the online environment. Even though they have discussion forums and are constantly engaged in discussions there, they say they still miss the actual human behind the computer. Adding the synchronous component and topping it off with an in-class flip makes students feel comfortable because it closely resembles a physical class. Students get to interact with one another, and they see the teacher. Also, they have to spend certain times in front of the computer to meet with the entire group, which adds to the feeling of actually being in class.

Use an In-Class Flip and Have a Teacher Support Station

Students can rotate through the different stations, but they also need to know there is one station where their teacher is waiting for them in case questions emerge. Even though in a regular online breakout rooms activity the teacher would be jumping into groups to provide this support, by adding the teacher support station, students might feel more freedom to talk and only search for the teacher when they need to.

As we have said throughout the book, in-class flipping is for everyone! For the face-to-face, the blended, and even the online educator. Don't be afraid to try these tips and to keep crafting amazing learning experiences for your students.

As we have shown in the various examples above, the in-class flip is not a single approach, but a variety of in-class configurations that allow flipped teaching to occur hand-in-hand with other teaching strategies.

REFLECTIVE PAUSE

Which of this chapter's strategies could you integrate into what you already do in your classroom? Do you feel ready for all of them?

Grab and Go Teaching Menu

READY TO TRY OUT AN IN-CLASS FLIP? We have prepared a special "menu" for you to explore, grab what you need, and put it into action in your teaching context. You will find a summary of all the chapter and key concepts in the book. You will also find a short description of important concepts and sections, along with the chapter and page where you can find them. All of this is in a grab and go format, so that you can quickly and easily find what you are looking for.

Chapter 1

What Is an In-Class Flip?   8–9

An in-class flip is a set of adaptable in-class configurations where the individual and group space coexist, allowing flipped learning to take place within the teaching setting.

The In-Class Flip vs. Blended Learning   9–11

An in-class flip is a set of adaptable in-class configurations where the individual and group space coexist, allowing flipped learning to take place within the teaching setting.

We present four practical, ready to use differentiation strategies: HyperDocs, Learning Menu, Choice Board, and Learning Path or Route.

Chapter 9

- Visualize the configuration.

- Plan your lesson carefully.

- Embrace the chaos.

- Always keep slower-paced students in mind.

- Start slowly.

- Complex content is great for in-class flipping.

- KISS: keep instructions super simple.

- Get feedback from your students.

- Get feedback from your colleagues.

- Always have a Plan B.

Chapter 10

Whether you decide to grade or not, accountability is a must for your students. Some of our favorite activities for this are: immediate response systems, sketchnoting, note-taking, testing, quizzing, experiments, the traffic light strategy, graphic organizers, and answer keys.

Chapter 11

Some common mindset challenges teachers face are their perception of discipline, resistance to relinquishing control, an incorrect perception of student abilities, and a lack of problem-solving skills. Other challenges include planning time, creating clear instructions, space, and student organization. Check out the different solutions to each problem in this chapter.

REFERENCES

Anderson, T., Rourke, L., Garrison, R., & Archer, W. (2001). Assessing teaching presence in a computer conferencing context, *Journal of Asynchronous Learning Networks, 5*(2), 1-17

Barnes, M., & Gonzalez, J. (2015). *Hacking education: 10 Quick fixes for every school* (Hack Learning Series). Cleveland, OH: Times 10 Publication.

Bates, T. (2016). Online learning for beginners. 1. What is online learning? tonybates. ca/2016/07/15/online-learning-for-beginners-1-what-is-online-learning/ Bergmann, J. & Sams, A. (2012) *Flip your classroom. Reach every student in every class every day*. Portland, Oregon: ISTE

Bergmann, J., Sams, A. & Gudenrath, A. (2015) *Flipped learning for English instruction*. Portland, Oregon: ISTE

Brinks-Lockwood, R. (2014) *Flip it! Strategies for the ESL classroom*. Michigan, US: University of Michigan Press.

Bondie, R., & Zusho, A. (2018). *Differentiated instruction made practical: Engaging the extremes through classroom routines*. Oxfordshire, UK: Routledge.

Borg, S. (2009). Introducing language teacher cognition. Retrieved from education. leeds.ac.uk/research/files/145.pdf

Buitrago, C.R. (2017) Making student-centered classrooms and letting go of control: Two great benefits of flipping. *Flipped Learning Today*. Pillar Corner. Fall, 2017.

Buitrago, C.R. (2018) My in-class flip about cybersecurity. (2018, June 26). crbuitrago. com/my-in-class-flip-about-cybersecurity/

Carbaugh, E. & Doubet, K. (2016) *The differentiated flipped classroom. A practical guide to digital learning*. Thousand Oaks, CA: Corwin

CAST. (2018). Principle: Provide multiple means of representation [website]. bit. ly/3wKiJXs

Coil, C. (2009) Flexible grouping: More than just moving their seats! Retrieved from http://www.carolyncoil.com/CCflexibleVA.pdf

Couros, G. (2015). *The innovator's mindset: empower learning, unleash talent, and lead a culture of creativity.* San Diego, CA: Dave Burgess Consulting.

Cox, J. (n.d.) Flexible grouping as a differentiated instruction strategy. Retrieved from: teachhub.com/flexible-grouping-differentiated-instruction-strategy

Coyle, D., Hood, P. & Marsh, D. (2010) *CLIL. Content and language integrated learning.* Cambridge: Cambridge University Press.

Fernández-Fontecha, A., O'Halloran, K. L., Tan, S., & Wignell, P. (2018). A multimodal approach to visual thinking: The scientific sketchnote. *Visual Communication, 18*(1), 5–29. doi.org/10.1177/1470357218759808

Flipped Learning Global Initiative. (2022). Flipped learning 3.0. www.flglobal.org/flipped-learning-3-0/ Gonzalez, J. (2014). Modifying the flipped classroom: The "in-class" version. edutopia.org/blog/flipped-classroom-in-class-version-jennifer-gonzalez

Hattie, J. & Yates, G. (2014) *Visible learning and the science of how we learn.* Oxfordshire, UK: Routledge

Highfill, L., Hilton, K. & Landis, S. (2016). *The HyperDoc handbook. Digital lesson design using Google apps.* Irvine: CA: EdTechTeam Press

Horn, M. and Staker, H. (2015). *Blended: Using disruptive innovation to improve schools.* San Francisco: Jossey-Bass

Infographics in the classroom teacher toolkit. California Academy of Sciences. (n.d.). Retrieved from calacademy.org/educators/infographics-in-the-classroom-teacher-toolkit.

Johnson, C. (2018) *Flipped 3.0 mastery learning: An insanely simple guide (Volume 1).* Irving, CA: FL Global Publishing

Jones, D. (2018) *Flipped 3.0 project based learning: An insanely simple guide (Volume 1).* Irving, CA: FL Global Publishing

Lyman, P. E. (2021). *The do-it-yourself escape room book: A practical guide to writing your own clues, designing puzzles, and creating your own challenges.* Skyhorse Publishing.

Marshall, H. & Kostka, I. (2020). Fostering teaching presence through the synchronous online flipped learning approach. *TESL-EJ Electronic Journal for English as a Second Language, 24*(2), Retrieved from tesl-ej.org/wordpress/issues/volume24/ej94/ej94int/

Marshall, H. & Rodriguez-Buitrago, C. (2017). The Synchronous Online Flipped Learning Approach. *TEIS News. The newsletter of the teacher education interest section.* TESOL. bit.ly/3MoidCW

Mazur, E. (November 12, 2020). Transform your teaching with Perusall. Webinar. mazur.harvard.edu/files/mazur/files/transform_teaching_nov_12.pdf

Ramirez, M. (May 30th, 2017) What's an in-class flip? martharamirez.com.co/blog/whats-an-in-class-flip/

Ramirez, M. (August 2, 2018) In-class Flip: teaching communication communicatively. martharamirez.com.co/blog/in-class-flip-teaching-pronunciation-communicatively/

Ramirez, M. (2018) In-class Flip: Flipping a literature class for student-centered learning. In J. Mehring & A. Leis (Eds), *Innovations in flipping the language classroom Theories and Practices.* (pp. 93-103). Singapore: Springer

Ramirez, M. (2021, January 17). Designing flipped instructions for differentiation [web log]. Retrieved from martharamirez.com.co/blog/designing-flipped-instructions-for-differentiation/.

Rohde, Mike (2013) *The sketchnote handbook: the illustrated guide to visual note-taking.* Berkeley, CA: Peachpit.

Sanchez Terrell, S. (2017). *Hacking digital learning strategies. 10 ways to launch edtech mission in your classroom.* (Hack Learning Series). Cleveland, OH. Times 10 publications.

Scrivener, J. 2005. *Learning teaching* (third edition). Oxford: Macmillan

Talbert, R. (2017). *Flipped learning: A guide for higher education faculty.* Sterling, VA: Stylus

Tomlinson, C. (n.d.). What is differentiated instruction. readingrockets.com

Tomlinson, C. (2014). *The differentiated classroom. Responding to the needs of all learners.* Alexandria, VA: ASCD

Tucker, C. (January 7, 2016) In-class flip: The flipped classroom meets the station rotation model. catlintucker.com/2016/01/inclassflip/

Tucker, C. (January 12, 2016) Free-form station rotation lesson. catlintucker.com/2016/01/free-form-station-rotation/

Tucker, C., Wycoff, T. & Green, J. (2017). *Blended learning in action. A practical guide toward sustainable change.* Thousand Oaks: CA. CORWIN A SAGE Publishing Company

Weinstein, Y., Sumeracki, M., & Caviglioli, O. (2019). *Understanding how we learn: A visual guide.* Routledge.

INDEX